Media
MINDFULNESS

Media Mindfulness

Educating Teens About Faith and Media

Gretchen Hailer, RSHM
Rose Pacatte, FSP

Saint Mary's Press®

We would like to dedicate this book with gratitude to all the pioneers in media literacy education in both the secular and religious communities, as well as people who may have been teaching media literacy without even knowing it.

 Genuine recycled paper with 10% post-consumer waste. 5109500

The publication team included Christine Schmertz Navarro, development editor; Lorraine Kilmartin, reviewer; Mary Koehler, permissions editor; prepress and manufacturing coordinated by the prepublication and production services departments of Saint Mary's Press.

Cover photo: Daniel Brunner/iStockphoto

Interior icons:
Paul Casper, pages 21, 44, 67, 77, 89, 99, 112, 112, and 123
Tinka Sloss, pages 32, 55, 89, and 123
FaithClipart, pages 32, 44, 55, 67, 77, 89, 99, 112, and 123
Daniel Brunner, chapter openers

ISBN 978-0-88489-905-1

Library of Congress Cataloging-in-Publication Data

Hailer, Gretchen.
    Media mindfulness : educating teens about faith and media / Gretchen Hailer and Rose Pacatte.
        p. cm.
Includes bibliographical references.
ISBN 978-0-88489-905-1 (pbk.)
    1. Mass media—Religious aspects—Catholic Church. 2. Mass media and teenagers. 3. Catholic Church—Doctrines. I. Pacatte, Rose. II. Title.
P94.H35 2007
261.5'208822—dc22

2006023865

Contents

Introduction

Throughout history, people have loved storytelling. From the first tales told around a campfire, to those illustrated on the walls of a cave, to words put down on paper with a quill and later multiplied by millions with a printing press, to photographs, films, and all forms of electronic media—radio, television, even interactive video games—we never pass up a good story. As followers of Jesus Christ, we are called to love the world today, and to live in freedom and responsibility. To do so means that we are to choose, critique, and analyze the sources of our stories, whether from news or entertainment, and to reflect on what they mean.

The Church's teaching on media and communications will be new for many of you. Yet herein you will find information to help you form and articulate your own criteria for stories and focus your own lenses for navigating your media world. You can then assist and mentor young people in navigating theirs. We will acquaint you with essential ideas about communication, media literacy education, and the four-step media mindfulness strategy for evaluating each medium.

The filmmakers, television executives, writers, marketers, photographers, and software developers of tomorrow are in our homes, pews, classrooms, and shopping malls today. Media mindfulness is no longer a suggestion; it is a pastoral imperative.

Media Mindfulness

What Is Media Mindfulness?

Media mindfulness is media literacy education in the context of faith formation.

Media Literacy Education

Media literacy education is essential for the twenty-first century. Sr. Elizabeth Thoman, CHM, founder of the Center for Media Literacy, and Tessa Jolls, the Center's president and CEO, wrote these words in the article "Media Literacy: A National Priority in a Changing World."

> The convergence of media and technology in a global culture is changing the way we learn about the world and challenging the very foundations of education. No longer is it enough to be able to read the printed word; children, youth, and adults, too, need the ability to critically interpret the powerful images of a multimedia culture. Media literacy education provides a framework and a pedagogy for the new literacy needed for living, working, and citizenship in the twenty-first century. Moreover, it paves the way to mastering the skills

7

required for lifelong learning in a constantly changing world. (Center for Media Literacy Web site, *www.medialit.org*)

We, the authors, affirm this educational statement. In *Media Mindfulness: Educating Teens About Faith and Media*, we apply the statement to faith formation. By anchoring media mindfulness in the media literacy education universe, we are able to mine its wonderful insights, its skill-building pedagogy, its theory and praxis, and integrate them into our ministries when we speak or teach about media and values, virtues, spirituality, theology, Catholic social teaching, morality, intentional living, prayer, and worship.

> "Media education is a quest for meaning. Much of the value of a quest lies in the search itself as well as in the achievement of the goal." (Worsnop, *Screening Images*, p. ix)

The Center for Media Literacy (CML; Web site at *www.medialit.org*) has developed a list of core concepts and key questions for media literacy education to help teachers, parents, teens, and children critically navigate the media culture of the twenty-first century. Media mindfulness, as a set of Christian life skills and a lifestyle, is rooted in these concepts. You will find these core concepts and key questions integrated throughout this guide.

The Pluses of Media Mindfulness

Teaching about media and values in public education can be difficult because of the pluralistic and relativistic moral, religious, and spiritual reality of our culture and because of the separation of church and state. Often, teaching about values can be done only in partnership with character and citizenship education. In addition, many secular educators shy away from the concept of "formation," which to them implies a lack of freedom in education.

We believe that the faith community can form

CML's Five Key Questions of Media Literacy

1. Who created this message?
2. What creative techniques are used to attract my attention?
3. How might different people understand this message differently than I do?
4. What values, lifestyles, and points of view are represented in, or omitted from, this message?
5. Why is this message being sent?

Five Core Concepts

1. All media messages are "constructed."
2. Media messages are constructed using a creative language with its own rules.
3. Different people experience the same media message differently.
4. Media have embedded values and points of view.
5. Most media messages are constructed to gain profit and/or power.

(Center for Media Literacy Web site *www.medialit.org*)

its members into free and responsible disciples while adhering to the highest standards of education and pastoral ministry. Therefore, media mindfulness allows us to interpret our culture's information and entertainment (storytelling) media in light of human and Gospel values, morality and spirituality, and the search for and discovery of meaning.

Concerns About the Media

There are several reasons why educators sometimes miss the opportunity to educate their students about media.

First, some adults do not see information and entertainment media as gifts of God; they perceive media perhaps as more of a problem than an asset in faith formation. In his 1957 encyclical letter *On Motion Pictures, Radio, and Television,* Pope Pius XII opens with this comment about modern technology in media.

> Those very remarkable technical inventions which are the boast of the men of our generation, though they spring from human intelligence and industry, are nevertheless the gifts of God, Our Creator, from Whom all good gifts proceed: "for He has not only brought forth creatures, but sustains and fosters them once created.[1]" (Introduction)

Second, many adults lack knowledge about the information and entertainment media. They see the popular culture these create but are unsure how to approach it from a faith perspective—one that respects and honors the opinions of young people.

Third, many adults prefer to control the media that children and teens consume, rather than communicating with them about media in the context of faith and values. They have the idea that antisocial or immoral media can cause like behavior in those who consume it. While research has produced interesting corollaries between media consumption and behavior, no one has been able to prove that watching television, for example, *causes* people to make certain choices or behave in certain ways. No researcher has established a *causal* link, though we know that media have the power to teach, to persuade, and influence us on many levels.

Responding Rather Than Reacting to the Media

Young children, of course, imitate in their play what they see around them. This is a way of learning. If they grow up in a positive environment, they will learn appropriate behavior and develop a sense of right and wrong from peers, older siblings, parents, other significant adults, and, from television.

What is an appropriate response, rather than a reaction, to media—media that Christian adults may judge inappropriate, immoral, or obscene for themselves and others? We do not consider media boycotts helpful. As media educators, we choose to educate parents, teachers, and young people in media mindfulness as the first and most powerful response we can make as people of faith in a "mediated" world.

Though writing letters expressing our views, both positive and negative, can be useful to advertisers and production companies, we believe that empowering others to choose media wisely and question everything they hear and see through media mindfulness is much more effective, influential, and long lasting.

Media Mindfulness is a tool for adults concerned with teaching young people about information and entertainment media in the context of faith. The book also provides background on various media for adults who are less familiar with them. Finally, the book provides tools that have been proven to help young people navigate the media world. Much as we might want to shield them from any sinfulness in the media, what we really want for them is the ability to recognize what they are seeing and hearing for what it is, and to form a Christian response to it.

Why *Media Mindfulness?*

Media Mindfulness is a comprehensive curricular tool created for adults who work with teens in Catholic high schools or parish youth ministry. With this resource, you can empower young people to understand and appreciate the fascinating world of media from the perspective of their Christian faith. With this knowledge, teens can make wise media choices, create meaningful media, and question and analyze what they do choose to watch, listen to, play, or read.

The Two Goals of This Book

This book has two goals. The first is to help you enhance your own understanding of media in a faith context so you can teach and encourage young people to do the following things:

- understand the role of the media culture in their lives
- recognize the difference between media values and gospel values
- learn about the two lenses that the strategy of media mindfulness utilizes
- develop inquiry skills needed to apply the "four questions" format to media choices
- become critically autonomous media consumers
- integrate faith and culture for an authentic Christian life and spirituality

The second goal of this book is to explore the theology and spirituality of communication and media. This book places media in the sacramental world created by God. The universe has the capacity to mediate God's grace as well as human sin. Once young people have the critical skills to discern appropriate media, they will have the tools to reflect, grow spiritually, and find meaning in ways that integrate faith and daily life.

Media Are Everywhere

Because media are all pervasive in our world, it would be irresponsible *not* to bring the media, their products and messages, into our teaching and learning about faith, morals, and values in the twenty-first century. Reading, writing, arithmetic, and religion are not the only navigational tools we need in the modern world. All of us need to read, write, and analyze the media as a cultural phenomenon—and to do so within all of these disciplines as well.

Many educators use film and television clips in their presentations to begin a conversation about subject matter, or play popular music cuts to illustrate core concepts of critical thinking about values and media. Sometimes teachers and youth ministers employ clips and cuts merely to attract the attention of young people.

We hope that by learning to engage with our communication and media culture in an informed

and faith-filled way, teachers, youth ministers, and young people—the media makers of tomorrow—can transform it for the good of humanity, imbued with human dignity and the spirit of Christ.

How Can You Most Effectively Use Media Mindfulness?

Become a Co-learner

The most important way for you to use this manual effectively is by becoming a knowledgeable co-learner about information and entertainment media. Each chapter provides significant background about a particular type of media. Having this knowledge and sharing relevant aspects of it with your students will give you a certain level of credibility with them. You can consider the information in each chapter as a kind of script to which you can refer.

This may be a new concept to you, but when it comes to media, the only way to be an effective teacher and minister is to be open to learning as much from young people as they will learn from you. This attitude will help you communicate about the medium effectively and engagingly, honoring the experiences and opinions of youth. At the same time, your respect and openness will invite them to bring their faith into their decisions and choices about the media they consume.

If you do not engage in media education as a co-learner, however, and present yourself as an expert, you are likely to lose any ground you might have gained. Teenagers know quite a bit about media. Learning *with* them is valuable because you not only let them share their own knowledge but also allow them to practice the media mindfulness techniques you are giving them. It is also important for you to experience *their* media, as well as those directed at your own age demographic, so you share some media experiences in common with them.

How to Use This Guide

This book is not simply for theology teachers or youth ministers. It is valuable for all faculty and staff in Catholic high schools as well as staff and volunteers in parish settings. This guide provides background for you and elements you can assemble for structured events, such as presentations or film festivals, or integrate into your existing plans. This book can be used in various ways. It can serve as a resource:

- **for a course or unit on media,** because the chapters are structured to let you customize your presentation for your audience and time frame
- **for media mindfulness across the curriculum,** as part of your regularly scheduled curriculum, or as scheduled media mindfulness events. Each chapter suggests ways to do this.
- **for contemplative prayer experiences** that bring faith and life together. Such opportunities enable youth to reflect more deeply and to build bridges between faith and life.
- **for a daylong or weekend retreat** to contemplate the seeds of the Gospel in mainstream media. The retreat could examine teens' awareness of the world around them and enable them to be mindful of stories, how they are told, how people are represented, their assumptions about human dignity, the good of the earth, the common good, and so on.
- **for parent and teacher association meetings** where participants analyze video clips of parents raising their children, or struggling to do so, and teachers teaching well or not so well. This book also helps you educate the young people's parents about the media mindfulness they are learning.
- **for enriching your media library of books, films, and music,** adding relevance to your teaching about media, communication, and culture in the faith community

- **for Total Parish Catechesis programs, the Rite of Christian Initiation for Adults (RCIA), or other sacramental preparation**

What Does This Book Contain?

The Structure of the Book

This book has ten chapters and six appendices. Chapter 1, "All About Media Mindfulness," is first of all for you, the teacher or youth minister. It creates the context for teaching about media in the faith community and surveys the background information you will need. This chapter is structured like the others but is intended to engage you before you begin media mindfulness sessions. It provides essential information and the strategies to help you introduce the topic of media mindfulness to your class or group.

In chapters 2 through 9, readers explore the world of eight particular media through the dual lenses of faith and mindfulness. Each chapter has the same structure: an introduction, a section with key facts about the medium, and several creative activities to do with young people.

Chapter 10 is intended to help integrate faith and life through the theology of communication and spirituality for Christians living in a world mediated by technology and messages.

Chapter Organization

In each of chapters 2 through 9, we approach one or several media through the lens of media mindfulness. The chapters are structured to let you choose elements that fit your needs.

- Each chapter begins with a "Scripture Connection" quotation and reflection that helps young people understand how God's word connects to their media world.

- The list of "Session Objectives" will help you decide the scope of your session. Do you wish to achieve all of these goals in one session, or will you choose just a few?

- In the "What Is . . . ?" and "Values" sections, we define each medium and list the values it tends to cater to in the commercial world. We list these because the values that media favor in our culture often do not coincide with human and Christian values. When we understand the values a particular medium tends to promote, it becomes easy to speak of contrasting Gospel values as criteria for choosing media programs.

- A brief history of each medium follows, along with a discussion of "how it works" as an industry. We encourage you to use this information in your presentation.

- A section on the Church's approach to each medium—or media in general—follows. You'll find quotations from ecclesial documents; these can help you frame ideas and give young people the faith language to communicate their own faith and values.

- The "Movies" section suggests related films, either for your own preparation or for group showing. Remember: always preview films in their entirety before showing them. A license may be required. (See appendix 4, "Fair Use of Media," for additional licensing information.)

- The "Characteristics" section summarizes some of the key features of the medium.

- The "Things to Remember When Talking with Teens" section suggests ways to co-learn with young people.

- "Media Saints and Greats," a kind of a Catholic trivia section, highlights saints who are patrons of various media—or who could be—and other relevant figures too. Not all are canonized, but all are strong role models. You may want to assign further research and reporting about these saints' relevance to their media and modern life, create saint games, or see movies about some of the saints, talking about them together afterward.

- "Media Detective" suggests ideas for homework, group work, research, and enjoyable ways to inquire, learn, and talk about faith, values, and media. You might offer small prizes to the sleuths who complete these tasks.

- Each "Activities" section outlines four exercises: a general group activity, a creative production in the medium under study, an alternative or supplementary exercise, and an activity that helps you apply the four-step media mindfulness analysis to the medium.

- At least two handouts related to the activities are included in each chapter.

- The "Cross-Curricular Connections" offer ideas for integrating the material into different subject areas. These ideas can heighten the young people's appreciation for a medium as social commentary and art form, as well as entertainment. Applying media mindfulness across the curriculum enriches the students' awareness of the media's social influence in every aspect of daily life, and links media mindfulness with all aspects of learning. The cross-curricular approach also provides opportunities for the creative teacher or leader to team teach, or allow for peer teaching.

- A brief "Reflective Exercise" and "Closing Prayer" end each chapter.

- Finally, you will be directed to a "Self-Evaluation" (appendix 6) where you can assess how the session unfolded, what you learned, and the effectiveness of your teaching methods.

We, the authors, hope and pray that *Media Mindfulness* will serve you effectively in the ministries you carry out so generously in the name of the Lord Jesus and his Church.

Chapter 1
All About Media Mindfulness

Introduction

Scripture Connection

> Blessed are your eyes, for they see, and your ears, for they hear. Truly I tell you, many prophets and righteous people longed to see what you see, but did not see it, and to hear what you hear, but did not hear it. (Matt. 13:16–17)

Our eyes and our ears perceive God's presence everywhere because God mediates God's self to us through creation and the people we live with. Media—our shared means of informing, entertaining, and storytelling—are also everywhere. God continues to speak to us through media in modern parables that are meaningful for our life's journey.

Session Objectives

This session will enable you to accomplish the following tasks and goals:
- To explore with young people the world of communication and the place of media in that world
- To explain what media literacy —and media mindfulness— are not
- To show the relationship of media mindfulness to media literacy education
- To consider the dual lenses of faith and mindfulness as ways to navigate the media culture
- To present the four-part media mindfulness strategy that will be used throughout this book

Media and Christian Values

People who create and promote media often value the following:	The Gospels value the following:
Immediacy • Youth • Newness	Patience • Dignity of all • Tradition
Bigness • Wealth • Success	Smallness • Poverty of spirit • Authenticity
Glamour • Consumerism	Ordinariness • Conservation
Disposability	Cherishability
Nature as a disposable commodity	Nature as God's gift
Complexity • Multitasking	Simplicity • Contemplation
Instant gratification • Winning	Discernment and choice • Integrity
The human body as an object	The body made in the image of God
A sense of entitlement	A sense of sufficiency

Things to Know About Media Mindfulness

It is our responsibility to be mindful of media because, like any form of communication, media tend to promote certain values—some that support the Christian life of discipleship, and others that do not. Mass media are at the heart of our culture, the primary means by which people communicate and interpret what matters. Media literacy education has become more common in the United States in the last few decades. Media mindfulness adds Gospel values to the media literacy approach, discerning God's presence in media stories and discovering what this reflection process means for us as disciples.

The word *media* is plural; each of its forms is a "medium." In English-speaking countries, the mass outlets for information and news are usually referred to collectively as "the media." The term *media* can thus be misleading. In reality, it embraces all technological forms of communication that "mediate" a message. There are many genres within each medium as well. Media mindfulness can be employed to focus on any medium and its productions as well as popular culture.

To build the foundation for a good understanding of media mindfulness, we begin with communication, the process by which values are shared.

Communication

Communication creates relationships between people. Through these relationships, we share our values with one another. The verb "to communicate" comes from the Latin *communicare* meaning "to participate, share, or hold in common." To communicate means to impart information or tell a story, and it can take several forms.

1. Intrapersonal communication, or "inner speech," is self-communication: a dialogue or conversation people have with themselves, especially when they need to make a decision.

2. Interpersonal communication is characterized by a mutual exchange of information or stories, usually between two people, either face to face or by telephone, instant messaging, e-mail, and so forth.

3. Group communication usually involves people gathered for a specific purpose, with specific goals in mind: perhaps to make a decision, carry out a task, resolve a situation, study a topic, celebrate, or pray.

4. Organizational communication is an absolute necessity for an association such as a business, government, nonprofit organization, or parish, to resolve conflicts and thrive. Information must flow continually from the top down, the bottom up, and across all departments or sections as well.

5. Media, or cultural and social communication, differ from the other forms. Note that the four forms above imply a "back and forth" dialogue. Media are delivery systems, and they generally deliver their content one-way. A single source, such as a television station or network, transmits to millions of sets at one time. The audience can receive the programming, but individuals cannot respond on equal footing. Mass media, mediated through technology, are often called "mass communications."

6. Extra-personal communication refers to communication between machines—machines operated by individuals, groups, and organizations. Examples include e-mail, instant messaging, and Web logs ("blogs" for short). Extra-personal communication has the potential to empower every person on earth and give a voice to each one.

Values Inform Communication

Whenever we have a conversation, our values are implicitly present because we communicate about what is important to us. In order to identify the values that media present to us, it is good to be aware of the values we bring to any encounter with media.

One easy way to uncover our values is to ask, Where do I put my time and money? This media-based exercise helps reveal our values and make ourselves accountable for them.

State Your Values

List the three main values that guide your life.
1.
2.
3.
The next time you watch a television show or a movie, reflect on your response to that "media product." Ask yourself: Why did I like or not like the show or film? How did my values influence my response? If you are aware of the values that are important to you and can articulate them, you will find they were probably affirmed or challenged in some way while you viewed the movie or show. It is healthy and necessary to touch base with our values as we engage and interact with media.

Values are important ideals that give direction and inspiration to our lives. Authentic values are those of the Gospel that foster human dignity and the common good. They help us build up the world around us. Self-centered values lead to negative attitudes and behaviors that are contrary to Gospel values and can cause people to suffer both spiritually and materially.

Culture

Culture exists because people communicate their values to one another, forming complex webs of relationship.

Pope John Paul II set the standard for understanding culture when he said:

"Culture . . . is a specific dimension of the existence and being of man. It creates among the persons within each community a complex of bonds, determining the interpersonal and social character of human existence. Man is both subject and creator of culture in which he expresses himself and finds his equilibrium." "Message of the Holy Father for the XVIII World Communications Day," no. 2)

We grow up immersed in our national culture. We soak in the values, attitudes, and beliefs of those around us and of the people we encounter through media. No matter how much a Mexican couple in the United States might want to raise their children as Mexicans, it just cannot happen. Such children will be influenced both by their Mexican parents and by the U.S. culture in which they live. Without other influences such as a healthy family life and faith, this local-environment culture can become a person's entire worldview, greatly influencing one's thoughts and actions.

Popular Culture

Moreover, every country has many subcultures. For example, U.S. military families have a unique culture because they may move frequently around the country and the world through their service. A larger subculture is the popular culture—the shared everyday experiences of ordinary people.

Though we cannot avoid the influence of this pop culture, we can increase our awareness of its pervasive messages. With awareness, we can discern which aspects of popular culture support Gospel values and which do not, which helps us escape the lure of the negative aspects. As Christians, our Baptism calls us not only to avoid but to challenge values that do not promote human dignity.

In this chapter, we will explore the popular culture that is the umbrella of the media culture. The relationships between the culture in general, media culture, and pop culture look like this:

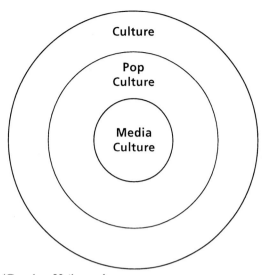

Culture

Pop
Culture

Media
Culture

(Gretchen Hailer et al.,
Believing in a Media Culture, p. 22)

What Is Media Literacy Education?

Media literacy education means teaching and learning about media, values, and the critical skills necessary for living in the twenty-first century. The media literate person is aware of the boundaries between reality and the constructed reality of the media and knows how to navigate them in meaningful ways.

Media literacy education has taken shape primarily in the last forty to fifty years. In 1964, John Culkin, SJ (1928–1993), wrote a curriculum on film study for his doctorate from Harvard; today he is known as the founder of the media literacy field in the United States. The Media Action Resource Center, formed by representatives from the national offices of Protestant denominations, developed the first comprehensive course about television in the United States in the late 1970s. This course, Television Awareness Training, has greatly influenced the media literacy movement.

The Center for Media Literacy (CML) was founded in 1977 with the publication of *Media & Values* magazine. Beginning about 1990, the media literacy education movement in the United States began to grow. Several international conferences were held in Canada and the United States during the next decade. In 2001, the Alliance for a Media

---

What Media Literacy Is *Not*

With the following list of ideas, let's distinguish media literacy from other literacies, and explore some of the basic elements of a comprehensive media education.

- Media "bashing" is *not* media literacy; however, media literacy sometimes involves *criticizing the media.*

- Merely producing media is *not* media literacy, although media literacy should include *media production.*

- Just teaching with videos or CD-ROMs or other mediated content is *not* media literacy; one must also *teach about media.*

- Simply looking for political agendas, stereotypes, or misrepresentations is *not* media literacy; there should also be an *exploration* of the systems that can make those representations appear "normal."

- Looking at a media message or a mediated experience from just one perspective is *not* media literacy, because media should be examined from *multiple positions.*

- Media literacy does *not* mean "Don't watch;" it means "*Watch carefully; think critically.*"

With thanks to Renee Hobbs, Chris Worsnop, Neil Andersen, Jeff Share, and Scott Sullivan

(Center for Media Literacy Web site, *www.medialit.org*)

Literate America was founded, which included an affinity group for faith communities.

People have become increasingly aware that they need skills to intentionally navigate the culture. Now, all fifty states have standards that include media literacy topics either as part of a standard subject such as English or social studies, or as a stand-alone curriculum unit.

The Two Lenses of Media Mindfulness

This book focuses on the media culture through two "lenses"—the lens of faith and the lens of mindfulness.

The belief that all of creation can reveal God to us is the first lens of media mindfulness. Priest and geologist Pierre Teilhard de Chardin, SJ, illustrated this Catholic teaching when he said, "By virtue of the Creation and still more, of the Incarnation, *nothing* here below is *profane* for those who know how to see" (*The Divine Milieu*, p. 66). This perspective encourages believers to see the world as a place full of wonder and awe, and the media as potential locations for discovering the presence of God in all manner of unlikely places. Using our eyes of faith on a daily basis keeps us rooted in the values of the Gospel, so that we may live the spiritual values of Jesus in everyday life and therein find meaning.

Mindfulness is the second lens, offering a reflective life strategy that questions and discerns. This lens allows us to study each medium in the context of its own structure and language. Using both of these lenses, believers can deepen their faith life in a mediated world in ways that are both faithful and relevant to twenty-first-century living.

The Strategy of Media Mindfulness

The media mindfulness strategy poses four questions for young people and adults to use with various types of media. These questions are based on the theological reflection process as well as the core concepts and key questions of media literacy education. Through the practice of theological reflection, a person moves from a basic awareness of an issue, to reflection, then to dialogue, and finally to action. These four questions are the tools that will help the students examine each medium through the lenses of faith and mindfulness:

- **What is going on?** What am I seeing, hearing, playing, reading, doing?
- **What is *really* going on?** What is the underlying device or technique that is being employed to accomplish the work of the particular medium, that is, to construct this other reality? Who pains and who gains from this particular media product? In whose interest is this message being communicated?

- **What difference does it make?** What Christian values, morals, or social issues does this media experience support or reject? What is the worldview behind it?
- **What difference can I make?** What personal or group response seems appropriate in light of my Christian beliefs?

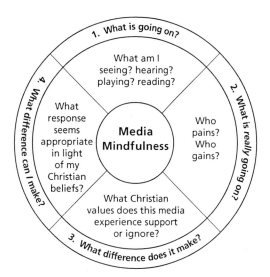

(Adapted from Gretchen Hailer et al., *Believing in a Media Culture*, p. 22)

The first two questions analyze the actual form and content of the media experience itself. The third question focuses on discernment, while the fourth invites a creative response from the believer. The questions are simple and can be used for personal reflection. Individual responses, when shared respectfully in twos and threes, can also generate fruitful conversations.

The strategy of media mindfulness not only influences our choice of media, it enables us to make meaning from what we actually choose to read, do, listen to, play, or watch. It is in this landscape of stories, using metaphor, analogy, and allegory, that the struggle for redemption and grace are won and lost, and, many times, won again. Although media mindfulness enables us to find meaning in all types of stories, the most satisfying stories are about characters who choose transcendent values to guide their decisions.

The Church and Media

The Church teaches that media are gifts of God that can be used to promote humanity as well as to lead people away from God.

Pope John Paul II's last written document was about the mass media. He released *The Rapid Development* on January 24, 2005. He wrote these words:

> The Church is not only called upon to use the mass media to spread the Gospel but, today more than ever, to integrate the message of salvation into the "new culture" that these powerful means of communication create and amplify. It tells us that the use of the techniques and the technologies of contemporary communications is an integral part of its mission in the third millennium.
>
> Moved by this awareness, the Christian community has taken significant steps in the use of the means of communication for religious information, for evangelization and catechesis, for the formation of pastoral workers in this area, and *for the education to a mature responsibility of the users and the recipients of the various communications media.* (No. 2, emphasis added)

The words in the last sentence of this excerpt articulate the heart of media mindfulness. It is our responsibility as pastoral leaders, teachers, and parents to help young people navigate our media world and become media mindful teenagers and adults.

Characteristics of Media Mindfulness

- creates autonomous critics who question the media and make wise choices about their media consumption when alone and when with others
- integrates faith and daily life
- promotes a pedagogy of respect for the opinions and insights of others, which can build community through dialogue

Movies About the Media

Use clips from these films to illustrate a point or begin a conversation, or show an entire film to your group and analyze it together.

Clueless (1995, 97 minutes, rated PG-13). In this pop-culture modernization of Jane Austen's *Emma,* Cher meddles in others' lives, and shopping becomes an emotional cure-all.

Dead Poets Society (1989, 128 minutes, rated PG). Set in a school for boys, this film stars Robin Williams as a gifted teacher. Use any of the scenes where Mr. Keating is teaching the boys about learning to think for themselves—for example, when he asks Mr. Dalton to stand on a desk and look at the world from a different point of view.

- is a vital life skill for the twenty-first century, an age increasingly characterized by mediated communication

Things to Remember When Talking with Teens About the Media

- Do anticipate that your students likely know more than you do about entertainment and information media and that during these sessions you will be co-learning with them. (See the introduction for an explanation of co-learning.)
- Do honor your students—their opinions, learning, and experience.
- Do listen actively to them; make eye contact to show your interest.
- Do avoid using imperatives such as "we must," "we have to," and "we need to," even though you will find this language in Church documents. Jesus *invites* and *calls* us to follow him by living the Commandments and Beatitudes.
- Do motivate students through inquiry, discovery, producing media, and sharing of experience about media, faith, and values. This approach is

always more effective than stressing information and rules.

- Do be fair towards media. If young people suspect you are "picking on" a particular medium, they will resist and ultimately tune you out.
- Do not put down their preferences or dislikes.
- Do not make generalizations about media.
- Do not pass judgment on any media you have not seen or heard personally.
- Do remember what it was like to be a teen.
- Do encourage inquiry and conversation about the media.

Media Saints and Greats

- **Saint Thomas Aquinas, OP** (1225–1274), was a philosopher, theologian, and teacher. His *Summa Theologica* explained all the main teachings of the Catholic Church at that time. No question was ever off limits for Saint Thomas, and for this reason he can be considered a patron saint of media mindfulness.
- **Blessed James Alberione, SSP** (1884–1971), founded ten religious congregations and associations, most dedicated to communicating the Gospel message through the media. He launched publishing houses and a film studio, and inspired the establishment of radio stations, video production centers, and Catholic bookstores in more than fifty countries. He encouraged an approach similar to media mindfulness among his congregation members.
- **Igino Giordani** (1894–1980) was a journalist who belonged to a lay association called the Focolare Movement, which is dedicated to spreading God's love to unite the world through the Gospel message. Giordani was exiled from Italy during Mussolini's fascist regime because he wrote against it.

Media Detective

Give these interesting and fun assignments to your students so they can investigate the media this week. Have them report back!

- Find out the most popular television shows for various audiences.
- Find out the top five movies at the box office.
- Find out what books are on the *New York Times* bestseller lists.
- Find out the top-selling CDs.
- Find out the most popular video games for teens.
- Find out the Vatican's Web address and describe the information it provides.
- Find out the number of annual awards for Catholic media of different types.
- Find out which award was given for excellence in the mainstream media most recently.

Activities

Activity 1: Communication Experiences

In this activity, students experiment with current means of communication—and older ones—to spark a conversation about the nature of more advanced technology. Follow these steps to prepare the exercise and share it with your group.

1. Before class, download the Pope's most recent document on communications and print it. (The document is issued every year on World Communications Day.) Highlight a few sentences that seem especially meaningful, put the document in an envelope, seal it, and address it to your class or group. Leave it in the rectory or school office for members from your class or group to pick up during the session.

2. Acquire two cell phones. Keep one and give the other to a student or group member and ask him or her to call you when you give the signal.

3. At the beginning of the session, explain that this exercise will illustrate communications "then" and "now." Ask for a volunteer to keep time. Then ask for two volunteers to go and get the letter and bring it back. After they leave, signal the person with the cell phone to call you and tell you how many people are present. Tell another student to announce it to the group. Have someone else call the weather line and announce the local conditions to the others.

4. When the students return with the letter, ask the timekeeper to announce how long it took to retrieve the letter, then ask a different volunteer to read the highlighted parts to the group.

5. Have the students discuss how they felt while they were waiting for the couriers to return. Ask these types of questions:

- What if surface or "snail mail" were the only long-distance communication available now?
- How would you feel about moving to a part of the world without electronic communication? What is the impact of such a lack in a world so much more technologically advanced?
- What are the benefits of swift communications? What might some negative aspects be? (Some examples include the "need for speed" and the increased demand for instant gratification.)

Activity 2: Creating Nonverbal Communication

In this activity, the game of charades stimulates reflection on nonverbal communication.

1. Prepare the group for a game of charades by reviewing the rules, including the signs for a book title, film, television show, song, quote, and any media form you wish to include. Explain that this particular game of charades will be limited to different forms of media.

2. Divide the group into two teams. Ask one person from each team to observe the team during the game and make notes about the kinds of communication that take place between same-team members, between team members and the person acting the charade, and between members of the opposing teams. Remind the observers to note nonverbal expressions, words, and body language. The observers will report back at the end of the game.

3. Ask another person to make a list of all the titles or phrases that were acted out.

4. At the end of the game, ask the two observers to report back on what they noticed regarding communication. Then ask the larger group to discuss these questions:

- What does the group notice about the charade items themselves?
- Do the items reflect school, home, church, or popular culture?
- What was interesting about the teams' ways of communicating?
- Were all of the forms of communication respectful?

5. Explain to the group that they have just experienced aspects of media mindfulness. First, the young people communicated about media (rather than simply consuming media). Second, there was a record of the media mentioned so that the group could reflect on the ideas the class had. Finally, there were two people observing the nature of the conversation, illustrating that communication can either support values of respect or challenge them.

Activity 3: Media List for College

In this activity, students come to a greater awareness of what media technology items they think are essential to them, and why.

1. Pass out a copy of handout 1–A, "Packing for College," to each student.

2. Instruct them to fill out the list of items and to give reasons for their choices.

3. After the students have completed their own lists, draw two columns on the board and ask the students to help you compile their lists. Invite them to give their reasons for listing the items.

4. When you have finished the list on the board, tell the students that the college they have selected will let them bring only two media items with them. Ask them to choose these two items from their own list. Then draw two more columns on the board and invite the group to share their results. Ask the students, Are you surprised by your choices? If so, why?

Activity 4: Learning to Be Media Mindful in a Visual World

Use this exercise to analyze a variety of billboards with your students. Prepare by taking digital photos of billboards the week before so you can project them on a screen during the session. Choose wide-ranging content: politics, alcohol, fast food, cars, public service, and so on.

Before showing students the billboards, give them each a copy of handout 1–B, "Media Mindfulness and Billboards." As a class, go through the four steps, using the additional questions for interpreting billboards. In addition, have students consider these questions:

- How close are some billboards to schools?
- What neighborhoods have billboards?
- How do these placements make an impact on their communities?

Reflective Exercise and Closing Prayer

Plan a visit to the parish church, a cathedral, or a monastery chapel. Ask the students to be silent as

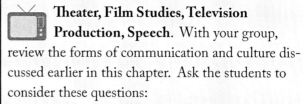

Cross-Curricular Connections

Theater, Film Studies, Television Production, Speech. With your group, review the forms of communication and culture discussed earlier in this chapter. Ask the students to consider these questions:
- What is the function of communication in each of these subject areas?
- How do sound and visuals function together to create meaning?

Economics, Civics, Government. Have students research the role of mass communications in each of these subject areas and describe their importance. Research the legislation regulating various media and analyze it for fairness in the service of the public interest.

Religion. Download *The Rapid Development*, by Pope John Paul II, from the Internet.
Copy it and read the document with your students. Talk about how the Pope understands God as expressed through his words on communication and culture.

they enter the building, to bless themselves with holy water, to reverence the altar, or to genuflect if the Blessed Sacrament is present.

Invite the group to take a contemplative walk around the church or chapel and to take note of the various ways God's Word is communicated. Point out that the symbols are present everywhere, even in how the building smells.

Ask the young people to remember one thing they notice. After ten or fifteen minutes, quietly gather together and sit in the chairs or pews. As the leader, sit behind the young people; play some soft sacred music from Taize or other sources. Read the following reflection as a guided meditation (or feel free to make up your own):

Lord, you have blessed us with the senses of sight, hearing, touch, taste, and smell so you can communicate your love and presence to us, so we can know you and live fruitfully in this world. In this, your house, we have seen the story of Creation, the fall from grace, our redemption, and we are offered the means of holiness through the sacraments and the example of your saints. Today, in this contemplative experience, you have communicated your love to me through _____. And now I invite each of us to share something that impressed us during our contemplative walk through this holy place.

Self-Evaluation

Please fill out a copy of handout appendix 6–A, "Self-Evaluation," in this manual.

Packing for College

You are about to leave for college. Use this form to help you decide what media technology to take with you for the year. Be sure to explain why you need each item.

Item	Why?
1.	
2.	
3.	
4.	
5.	
6.	
7.	
8.	
9.	
10.	

Media Mindfulness and Billboards

(This diagram is adapted from *Believing in a Media Culture,* by Gretchen Hailer, Thomas Zanzig, and Marilyn Kielbasa [Winona, MN: Saint Mary's Press, 1996], page 38. Copyright © 1996 by Saint Mary's Press. All rights reserved.)

Chapter 2

Popular Culture and Media Mindfulness

Introduction

Scripture Connection

> Therefore I tell you, do not worry about your life, what you will eat or what you will drink, or about your body, what you will wear. Is not life more than food and the body more than clothing?
>
> Therefore do not worry, saying, "What will we eat?" or "What will we drink?" or "What will we wear?" For it is the Gentiles who strive for all these things; and indeed your heavenly Father knows that you need all these things. But strive first for the Kingdom of God and his righteousness, and all these things will be given to you as well. (Matt. 6:25; 31–33)

In these passages from the Sermon on the Mount, we notice how simply Jesus challenges us not to "sweat" what he sees as the small things of life. Many of the details we worry about are essentially *wants*, not *needs*. We all *need* to eat and drink and be clothed, but we do not *need* the latest fad foods or energy drinks or name brand clothing! These are often *wants* induced by advertising and peer pressure. Once we learn to differentiate wants from needs, and to determine the real source of our desires, then we can enjoy the popular culture with the true freedom of the sons and daughters of God.

Session Objectives

This session will enable you to accomplish the following tasks and goals:
- to help young people differentiate between needs and wants
- to assist them in exploring various aspects of the popular culture
- to explain to them that the allure of pop culture can be dangerous
- to have them consider the Church's view of popular culture
- to have them apply the strategy of media mindfulness to popular culture

---

What Is Popular Culture?

Popular culture, or pop culture, is the "people's culture" that prevails in any given society. Its nature is determined by the daily interactions, pursuits, needs, and wants that make up the everyday lives of ordinary people. Pop culture encompasses many practices, including those pertaining to food, clothing, body adornment, slang, jokes, and mass media entertainment such as sports, TV, and popular music.

Those who create and promote popular culture generally value the following.

- instant popularity
- disposable things
- cultivating followers
- consumerism
- body image
- what is current
- what is noticeable
- what is "here today and gone tomorrow"

Things to Know About Popular Culture

Popular culture exerts a tremendous influence over us, whether we are aware of it or not. Popular culture, with its changing genres, is at once amusing and alluring. It is the stuff of informal banter in the cafeteria and chatter during class breaks in the halls. It is the visual joke sent to others by e-mail or the verbal joke circulated by word of mouth. It is the latest fad in fashion, toys, cars, or sports.

It is necessary to give proper attention to the subtle messages of the pop culture, and the mass media environment that delivers them, in order to resist the attitudes and behaviors that are contrary to the Gospel. Though many cultural values and practices may be in line with Christian beliefs, we are called by our Baptism to be "countercultural," to stand for strong values that in some cases are very different from the secular values the popular culture holds up to us daily.

Three important areas of popular culture are body image, food and drink, and sports. These are among the major genres of teen popular culture. As you already know, pop fads can come and go, then reappear in the same or other forms decades later. Sometimes we hear parents or grandparents exclaim, "I can't believe that fashion is back in!"

Body Image

The culture influences and is influenced by the way people view and take care of their bodies.

Body image trends are fascinating: they change from culture to culture, century to century, even decade to decade. Changing criteria for female beauty, for example, can best be seen in the history of art. The Dutch artist Rembrandt van Rijn (1606–1669) painted pictures of the most beautiful women of his day, who were voluptuous, round, and sensual. Similarly, the French Impressionist painter Pierre-Auguste Renoir (1841–1919) depicted "meaty" nudes stepping out of the bath.

In the 1950s and '60s, the archetypal, iconic *femme fatale* was Marilyn Monroe (1926–1962). Marilyn wore a size 12. She had a tummy, thighs, and a soft neck and arms. Her image was quite different than the very slim, high fashion "waif look" later popularized by designer Calvin Klein in the form of his favorite model Kate Moss, who wore a size 0 at one point.

What happened to create this shift in the culture's perception of female beauty? Women decades ago likely made great efforts to emulate Marilyn Monroe's beauty and style. So why have women (and men) gone from accepting a curvaceous form to pursuing a youthful yet almost gaunt image? Has the media's ideal of beauty led many people to try to lose weight by all manner of dieting, exercising, liposuctioning, and obsessing over every wrinkle and gray hair?

The profit motive, rather than medical knowledge, bears quite a bit of responsibility. There has been a rapidly increasing economic drive in America since the 1950s to market nearly any product likely to make money, regardless of its human impact. So it is no coincidence that corporations increased their focus on female adolescents and women, who were a vast untapped market. Some advertisers then had to create a discontent, a perceived need, in order to sell products. Over time, advertisers and corporations created a new model of female beauty: the eternally young and slim woman. This would be in contrast to companies who have actively promoted greater health in women through exercise, healthy eating, and education.

Many forces came together to change the culture's notion of beauty. This image of female beauty is exemplified in the form of the Barbie doll, released in 1959. Barbie is the fantasy girl who has been accused of planting the seeds of body-image discontent in little girls. The billion-dollar diet industry took root as fashion magazines began to picture impossibly skinny models scowling seductively from their pages. What most readers failed to realize, however, was that the "look" in magazines was achieved mostly by airbrushing and lighting!

Many Americans have bought into these marketing campaigns and as a result, they now spend billions of dollars a year on diets and diet-related services. Eating disorders such as anorexia nervosa and bulimia among youth—especially young women—increased along with this quest to become thin. Both conditions require medical attention, can cause permanent damage to health, and may even lead to death. In search of the perfect body, many young women also demand cosmetic surgery at a time when their bodies have not yet matured to their full potential.

Skin Fashions

Popular culture also promotes "skin fashions," such as certain skin tones, cosmetics, tattooing, and body piercing, as well as hairstyles. These vary from decade to decade, culture to culture. All of these fads can tap into people's desire and perceived need to belong to a group.

Historically, people in various ethnic groups have held clear preferences for skin color, often favoring those with light tones over dark. Oddly enough, in some societies, people often strive for a "tan" appearance, even though for some people a darkened hue is really evidence of skin damage and a sign of early aging or even cancerous conditions. Other societies (some in Asia, for example) favor skin that is kept from the sun or even lightened through various methods.

People have used cosmetics for centuries to enhance skin tone and facial features. As early as

4000 BC, the Egyptians were using various barks, herbs, and berries to color eyes and skin in ways that resemble eye makeup and blush today. Interestingly enough, it wasn't until the 1920s that ordinary American women—not just actresses and prostitutes—began to use lip color and nail polish.

Tattooing communicates status in certain cultures. Sons of Samoan chiefs are privileged to have elaborate tattoos etched on their bodies. In past decades, United States servicemen, particularly those in the Navy, had themselves tattooed during their travels. Because these men visited exotic ports, the lure of the tattoo was understandable.

Body piercing is another skin fashion that appears from time to time in various cultures. In traditional Mexican families, baby girls have their ears pierced at the time of their presentation to God. Recently, men and women throughout North America have been piercing other parts of the body to hold rings and other jewelry.

Facial and body hair also have cultural "seasons." In ancient times, before the razor, men removed facial hair with shells—a good enough reason to maintain beards! As the centuries unfolded in Western culture, vogues developed for certain hairstyles for both men and women. Usually, elaborate hairstyles for women were only *de rigeur* for the upper classes and often took hours to do.

Until the last century, body hair was usually left alone, but during World War II when silk stockings were hard to find, women began to shave their legs and use eyebrow pencil to draw "seams" down the back of them. Soon after, as bathing suits became more revealing, women also shaved the hair under their arms. Today, the popular culture sells body waxing as "sexy" and many women and men have their body hair removed. This last fad also has its dangers since our body hair serves important functions for good health and hygiene.

Body fragrances also have been around for millennia. The ancient Greeks and Romans used scented oils after their elaborate bathing rituals. The fragrances came from tree bark, berries, floral essences, herbs, and spices, with alcohol as a stabilizing ingredient. Today the perfume and cologne industry garners revenues in the billions, and another product has more recently emerged: body sprays. These are lighter than perfumes and colognes, and are marketed for after-shower use. The targeted customers for these products are young males.

Clothing

Clothing fashions that were once culturally localized are now global commodities, with clothing often sewn in faraway countries. It is in the clothing industry that we can really see the necessity of separating our wants from our needs.

We may, for instance, need a new pair of sneakers. But do we need a pair that costs over a hundred dollars? This is where the marketers step in. Since popular culture often favors "planned obsolescence," it becomes necessary to create ever newer styles of shoes and other clothing to lure us. (Planned obsolescence is a marketing strategy that anticipates a short life span for a product: it will be obsolete, outworn, or out of style soon and will need to be replaced.)

People can end up with large wardrobes if they buy new clothes every time the fashion changes. Sometimes designers stress the sleek look—tight clothing meant to show no bulges at all. At other times the cuts are bulky and chunky—a perfect style for those who haven't dieted themselves into a size 0. For one season, a drab color is in; at another time, flashy colors are all the rage. The one thing to remember, though, is this: in order to be "in," to belong, adults as well as young people feel the need to buy what is "in" and what is cool.

The mall, the ubiquitous shopping center, fulfills the need to belong in a new way. The first of the now-traditional American shopping malls appeared in Dallas in 1931. Its design had all the stores facing each other, but with their backs to the outside world. This layout is the opposite of the time-honored "Main Street USA" whose storefronts line the open street. Today, many of the former "mom

and pop" businesses found in town centers can no longer compete with the huge chain department and specialty stores in the malls. Though small businesses have long been the backbone of the United States economy, today many cannot compete. They close their doors on Main Street for good once the local mall or megastore is constructed.

On a positive note, malls also provide a place for people of various ages and lifestyles to hang out. Often when we visit a mall, we'll see some of the following individuals and groups: young couples enjoying their small children tumbling in the play area; older singles reading a book or newspaper over a cup of coffee; middle-aged people using the mall for a safe exercise venue; teens cruising by foot to check out their peers.

Food and Drink

Another highlight of the mall is the food court. In the past, food had specific cultural and geographic boundaries, but in this age of globalization, fast-food outlets literally dot not only the mall but also the globe. Health professionals keep reminding us that a regular diet of these foods is simply not good for us. Small children raised on french fries, for example, are much more apt to have problems with obesity as teens and high cholesterol as adults.

In addition to the ever-present diet soft drinks, advertisers are now promoting so-called "energy drinks" through billboards, magazines, and product placement on television and in films. This campaign may simply be a scheme of the soft drink industry to sell to a youth audience something they already possess—in abundance.

On a positive note, many Americans are trying to eat in a healthier way, dieting for health rather than for fashion, and moving toward organic foods and away from foods that have a high chemical content. These are trends that respect human dignity and the environment.

Sports

Sports create a sense of belonging that is an important part of human experience. Athletics help keep people healthy, and team sports promote personal growth and build community. We cheer for "our" team no matter who they are, and we purchase all manner of attire to express our allegiance. Watching live games, or televised ones at home, brings friends and family together. Sports also have a global dimension: we can watch soccer games from all over the world and follow the careers of international players with just a click of the remote.

Sports are an important aspect of the popular culture. Not only do they create celebrities, but they are an industry as well. When we see how professional teams lure graduating college players with huge salaries, we can see how money dominates in professional sports.

Church and Popular Culture

The 2006 *National Directory for Catechesis (NDC)* from the United States Conference of Catholic Bishops acknowledges that "much of what people today know and think about is conditioned by the various means of mass communications" (page 105). The Church expresses the sense that media are gifts from God and that all believers should engage in the media culture that surrounds us—and engage with a discerning eye. The Church must use media tools available to communicate the Good News and must also teach the young, especially, to recognize the consumerism and other un-Christian values that the media can communicate.

In 1992 the Pontifical Council for Social Communications issued *Dawn of a New Era (Aetatis Novae)* and called for a critical and mindful engagement with popular media and the culture it produces:

> But even as the Church takes a positive, sympathetic approach to media, seeking to enter into the culture created by modern communications in order to evangelize effectively, it is necessary

at the very same time that the Church offer a critical evaluation of mass media and their impact upon culture. (No. 12)

In his 2005 apostolic letter *The Rapid Development*, Pope John Paul II expresses this hope:

> In fact, the Church is not only called upon to use the mass media to spread the Gospel but, today more than ever, to integrate the message of salvation into the "new culture" that these powerful means of communication create and amplify. It tells us that the use of the techniques and the technologies of contemporary communications is an integral part of its mission in the third millennium. (No. 2)

The 2006 *NDC* from the United States Conference of Catholic Bishops synthesizes relevant documents and articulates their teaching for the faithful in the United States. The *NDC* acknowledges the popular culture in which young people live, and from which they often derive values contrary to those of the Gospel:

> Catholic young people, like their counterparts in other faith traditions, have emerged as principal consumers of a developing popular culture that emphasizes a level of materialism and permissiveness designed to sell products and entertainment to the greatest number as efficiently as possible. (P. 16)

Characteristics of Popular Culture

- catches people's attention
- creates trends
- determines fashion
- is stylish
- is "all the rage"
- is "cool"
- creates artificial needs

Movies About Popular Culture

Use clips from these films to illustrate a point or begin a conversation, or show an entire film to your group and analyze it together.

Clueless (1995, 97 minutes, rated PG-13). In this pop-culture modernization of Jane Austen's *Emma*, Cher meddles in others' lives, and shopping becomes an emotional cure-all.

Simply Irresistible (1999, 94 minutes, rated PG-13). In this fable, a young woman inherits a restaurant from her mother. But she cannot cook and wants to sell the restaurant because it is neither popular nor profitable, and she questions how she fits into the role that has been given her.

Robots (2005, 91 minutes, rated PG). This animated film portrays the story of robots with aging parts combating a corporate effort to replace all old parts with upgrades.

Super Size Me (2004, 100 minutes, rated PG-13) In this documentary, a man eats only at McDonald's for a month and lives to tell the story of fast food's effects on his health, work performance, and relationships.

Things to Remember When Talking with Teens About Popular Culture

- Do remind the students about the pervasiveness of pop culture.
- Do not put down their pop culture choices.
- Do ask them why they wear certain fashions.
- Do not judge their motives in engaging in popular culture.
- Do explain the possible dangers in some aspects of pop culture.

Media Saints and Greats

Venerable Pierre Toussaint (1766–1853) was a married man from Haiti, once a slave, who became a famous hairdresser in New York City. He is buried there in Saint Patrick's Cathedral.

Saint Pascal Baylon (1540–1592) was a Spanish Franciscan brother who was a hospitable doorkeeper and excellent cook.

Saint Vitus (third to fourth century) was a Sicilian martyr. A cult arose around him that included dancing in front of his statue to invoke healing from various diseases.

Activities

Activity 1: A Mall Crawl

In this activity students experience a shopping mall on a number of levels as people of faith.

1. Gather a small group of students at a mall.

2. Divide the group into pairs. Give each two-person team notepads, pencils, and $100 in fake mall cash. (You can find play money in a toy store, or easily create some pretend bills.)

3. Ask team members to circle the mall once alone, in silence, noting what they see, hear, and feel, observing the storefronts without going in. Tell them to just *be* in the mall as opposed to trying to "get the point." Just have them notice the people, the stores, the products, the advertising, and the sounds.

4. Suggest that the teams meet at a designated spot for a cold drink in about forty minutes to share their findings.

5. After this check-in and sharing, invite the teams to go into the stores to notice the fashions, where they are made, the window dressings, color, target audiences, and to decide what they want to buy with their fake mall money. Have the teams note this information down. Suggest that they

Media Detective

Give these interesting and fun assignments to your students so they can investigate the media. Have them report back!

- Find out what the "in" slang words are.
- Find out what the latest food fad for teens is.
- Find out what the coolest energy drink is.
- Find out what it means to be an anchor store at the mall.
- Find out which U.S. clothing label has the longest history in the marketplace.
- Find out what awards allow the American public to recognize their favorite performers.
- Find out which cable channel gives annual awards for movie videos.

briefly interview shoppers and store employees about why they are there in the mall, and jot down their answers.

6. Finally, have the whole group gather to discuss their experiences, referring to the notes they have taken.

7. Close by praying about the experience.

Activity 2: Product Design and Labeling

In this activity, students experience the process of product design and labeling.

1. Divide the group into boys-only and girls-only pairs.

2. Pass out copies of handout 2–A, "Product Design and Labeling." Ask the girls' pairs to design an article of clothing or accessory for females and ask the boys' pairs to design an article of clothing or accessory for males. (Note that the clothing can be attractive but should be appropriate, in other words, no lingerie or other types of underwear.)

3. When they have finished their designs, have each pair of girls exchange designs with a pair of boys. Instruct the pairs to create a label or trademark for the clothing or accessory the other team designed.

4. When everyone has finished, have each team of four explain its designs and labels to the entire group. Have the group vote for the item and label they like best.

Activity 3: Target Marketing

This activity helps young people better understand the process of target marketing for mass consumption.

1. Ask the students to form groups of three to brainstorm the names of at least thirty existing brands, regardless of target audience, and write them down: clothing, shoes, cars, sports equipment, food and drink, and so on.

2. Now ask them to devise target market categories and have them classify the brands accordingly. Examples of target markets might be "people who love science" or "sports fans."

3. Invite each small group to share its results with the entire group. Encourage clarifications and comments.

4. Try to come to some group consensus regarding the exercise.

Activity 4: Applying Media Mindfulness to Popular Culture

In this activity, the young people apply the strategy of media mindfulness to popular culture.

1. Distribute copies of handout 2–B, "Media Mindfulness and Popular Culture," to the young people.

2. Ask them to individually choose one aspect of popular culture to examine. Have the students apply the media mindfulness strategy on the handout to that aspect of pop culture.

3. After giving the students sufficient time for their reflection, ask them to share their findings with another student.

4. Encourage open conversation in the large group, using the outline of the media mindfulness strategy to talk about the different aspects of pop culture. You may want to begin by asking, "What part of this chart impressed you the most, and why?"

Cross-Curricular Connections

 Geography and Social Studies. Have the students find the location of the largest malls in the United States; make certain they find out what stores are there as well.

History. Have a discussion about current clothing fashions and other decades when similar fashsions were popular in the United States.

Reflective Exercise

Create a quiet setting. Have the students gather in a large group. Pass out items to each student that represent the popular culture (cell phones, energy drinks, soda cans, T-shirts, fast-food containers, celebrity magazines, jewelry, clothing, shoes). Ask them to ponder the items and then invite anyone who wishes to offer a short prayer about the item in light of the "God meaning" (where they see God) in the item.

Closing Prayer

Shopper God, you are always in the sacred mall of our hearts searching out our wants and needs. Give us the strength to ask you for what we need, and if we do not know what it is, help us discover it in our silence before you. Amen.

Self-Evaluation

Please fill out a copy of appendix 6–A, "Self-Evaluation," in this manual.

Product Design and Labeling

Part 1: Team Member Names	Part 2: Team Member Names
Design a clothing item or accessory.	Design a label for the clothing item or accessory.

Media Mindfulness and Popular Culture

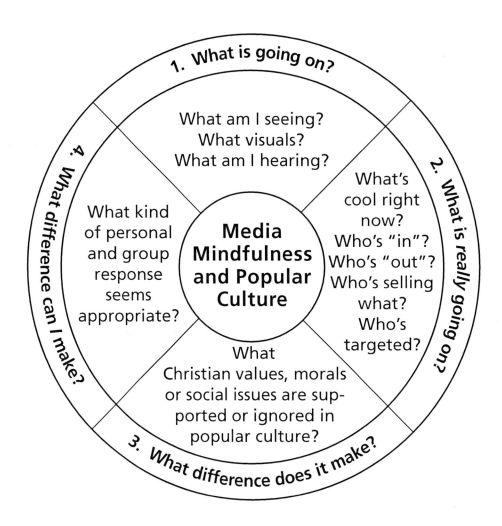

1. What is going on?

2. What is really going on?

3. What difference does it make?

4. What difference can I make?

What am I seeing? What visuals? What am I hearing?

What's cool right now? Who's "in"? Who's "out"? Who's selling what? Who's targeted?

What Christian values, morals or social issues are supported or ignored in popular culture?

What kind of personal and group response seems appropriate?

Media Mindfulness and Popular Culture

(This diagram is adapted from *Believing in a Media Culture*, by Gretchen Hailer, Thomas Zanzig, and Marilyn Kielbasa [Winona, MN: Saint Mary's Press, 1996], page 38. Copyright © 1996 by Saint Mary's Press. All rights reserved.)

Chapter 3

Advertising and Media Mindfulness

Introduction

Scripture Connection

> The eye is the lamp of the body. So, if your eye is healthy, your whole body will be full of light. (Matt. 6:22)

It is very important to develop a discriminating inner vision. Jesus reminds his listeners, then and now, that a healthy inner vision gives us the discernment tools we need to interact with the world around us and make meaningful choices in our lives.

Session Objectives

This session will enable you to accomplish the following tasks and goals:
- to assist young people in understanding the purpose of advertising
- to provide them with a brief overview of the history of advertising
- to invite them to examine some techniques used in advertising
- to challenge them to apply media mindfulness to commercial ad messages

What Is Advertising?

Advertising is the public promotion of a product or service through some form of media.

The advertising industry generally values the following:
- the creation of artificial needs—often by making wants seem like needs
- demographics with purchasing power
- a consumer mentality
- the catchy over the ordinary
- the glitzy over the plain

Things to Know About Advertising

Advertising is more than the simple promotion of products or services. As implied by its Latin root *advertere*, meaning "to turn toward," advertising actually fuels the business of media culture, encouraging consumers to look toward a product and then buy it. In European countries and elsewhere, people refer to advertising as propaganda, which is information spread for the purpose of promoting some product or cause. As Americans, we tend to reserve the word *propaganda* for political contexts. Whatever we call it, and whether its approach is direct or subtle, advertising aims to turn our attention toward a product, look, and buy.

Advertising is a global business, and a multi-billion-dollar industry in the United States. All we have to do is note the price of a 30-second TV commercial during the annual Super Bowl to have a clue about the extraordinary amounts of money generated by the business. Remember, advertising agencies have one goal and one goal only: to sell a product. Many products sell themselves because of their quality and value. But keeping consumers constantly dissatisfied with what they currently possess so that they will turn toward something new is a common advertising technique.

A Brief History of Advertising in the United States

From its newspaper-based origins, advertising has expanded in three centuries to include magazines, signage and billboards, broadcast radio and television, cable channels such as MTV, the Internet, and other electronic means.

The Early Years of Advertising

In 1704, the *Boston News-Letter* printed America's first newspaper advertisement, an announcement seeking a buyer for an estate in Oyster Bay on Long Island. Benjamin Franklin's *General Magazine* printed the first American magazine ads in 1742.

A century later, in 1841, Volney Palmer opened the nation's first advertising agency in Philadelphia. An early example of the advertising "blitz" strategy occurred in 1850 when Phineas T. Barnum brought Jenny Lind, the Swedish Nightingale, to New York for her American singing debut. He employed newspaper ads, handbills, and broadsides to drum up interest for the event; so much so that 30,000 New Yorkers lined up on the docks to welcome her!

The first advertisement for Smith Brothers Cough Candy Drops appeared in 1852 with the word *trademark* on the packaging. In a humorous turn of events, the public mistakenly named the Smith brothers in the illustration Trade and Mark, which of course were not their real names. Smith Brothers Cough Drops, some in the traditional licorice flavor, are still sold today in packaging that reflects its original design. This company was the first to use a trademark on its packaging.

Advertising in the Nineteenth Century

By 1861, there were twenty ad agencies in New York City, most of whom placed advertising not only in newspapers but in magazines as well. In 1878, J. Walter Thompson bought out William J. Carlton's small ad agency and renamed it after himself. JWT is the oldest American ad agency still in existence.

In 1884, the invention of the linotype machine advanced the use of color in printing. This era saw the debut of *Ladies' Home Journal*, *Life*, and *Cosmopolitan* magazines. By linking color printing with magazines directed to women, advertising began its journey into the flashy use of color and slogans, an approach that is still popular in the industry today.

In 1880, Philadelphia department store mogul John Wanamaker hired John E. Powers to bring a new style of advertising to his enterprise. Powers's honest, direct, and fresh appeal emphasized products' style, elegance, and comfort. He also let consumers know that if they were not completely satisfied with the product, their money would be "cheerfully refunded." Powers was later called the father of honest advertising.

Government and Advertising

By the mid-1800s, in response to the high volume of advertising painted outdoors on billboards, boulders, barns, and other urban and rural buildings, several states began to impose limitations to protect natural scenery from sign painters. In 1906, at the federal level, Congress passed the Pure Food and Drug Act, forcing product labels to list the product's active ingredients. In 1914, the Federal Trade Commission (FTC) Act was passed, and Joseph E. Davies was named the first FTC chairman. Section 5 of the Act allowed the Commission to issue cease-and-desist orders against dishonest advertising. In 1926, the Better Business Bureau was organized to prevent advertising scams. It still carries on that mandate nationwide.

The Evolution of Modern Advertising

Much of the character of our present-day advertising emerged in the first half of the twentieth century. In 1911, Woodbury Soap began its "A Skin You Love to Touch" campaign in the *Ladies' Home Journal,* an early use of sex appeal in American advertising. By 1923, National Carbon Company's *Eveready Hour* was the first regularly broadcast entertainment program to be sponsored by an advertiser on radio. By 1938, advertisers were spending more dollars on radio than magazines. Television was the obvious next step. With 7,500 television sets in New York City, NBC aired the first TV ad spot in 1941, featuring a Bulova watch that ticked for sixty seconds. Even with this static, magazine-like ad, television positioned itself early to usurp radio and print as the leading outlet for advertising messages. In 1981, when MTV debuted with its music videos, few would foresee that its style of music videos would revolutionize the design of TV commercials.

At the turn of this past century, the Interactive Advertising Bureau reported that Internet advertising revenues in the United States totaled $8.2 billion; by 2005, the total was $12.5 billion. Following the leadership of Procter & Gamble, the advertising industry moved to standardize the way it measured Internet advertising in the *Interactive Audience Measurement and Advertising Campaign* *Reporting Guidelines.* The guidelines have both a U.S. and a global version.

How Advertising Works

The advertising industry is a feature of a capitalist economic system, and competition is built into its own practices as well. Ad agencies compete with one another to contract with companies that want to sell a product or service. This next section briefly describes how the business of advertising works.

The Advertising Company's Work

A company's representatives approach an advertising firm because they seek ways to boost demand for an existing product or service, or to launch a new one. A creative advertising team from the firm then pitches an ad campaign to the company representatives. The pitch often includes perks such as expensive dinners, sports tickets, and the like.

The agency that wins the contract then handles all aspects of the ad campaign. They research the market to target desirable audiences, design the various components of the campaign, write scripts or scenarios for commercials, hire artists and actors, design print materials, and buy media space or time in a variety of media.

Demographics in Advertising

An essential focus for advertisers, demographic analysis classifies groups by characteristics such as age, gender, ethnicity, income, and education. Marketing companies often position personnel in shopping malls and elsewhere to ask people about their buying habits or to actually look at product displays and taste food products.

As a result of this research, the various elements of the marketing plan are put into place. Before finalizing it, the company assesses how best to spend its advertising dollars. Let's say that a desirable target group for a certain product is young

African American and Hispanic males. The advertiser would then buy advertising time on the television programs that many young Hispanic or African American males like to watch. (Companies like the Nielsen Media Research and Arbitron Radio Research provide demographic information to advertisers.) Advertisers might place billboards in neighborhoods with high concentrations of those men, or they might use relevant cultural or language references or choose appropriate celebrities as spokespersons.

Often the agency gathers what are called focus groups to see if their strategies are effective. In a focus group, a sampling of a target audience gives feedback about specific advertising ideas. If members of the intended demographic group indicate that the ads are not on track, the agency adjusts or perhaps redesigns parts of the campaign accordingly.

The "Media Blitz"

Advertisers may use a variety of media simultaneously in a single campaign. Such a "media blitz" might include TV commercials, Internet pop-up ads, magazine and newspaper spreads, radio spots, product placement in films, new packaging, and promotional giveaways and contests. Advertisers pass much of the cost of all advertising (including marketing and promotion) to the consumer: in some cases up to 55 percent of a product's retail price pays for advertising.

Advertising educates consumers about the products they may want to buy—those that solve customers' problems or enhance customers' lives. But advertising can also create a need where none existed before, and advertisers also use numerous techniques to influence consumers. For example, in the old days of advertising when the circus came to town, it paraded through the streets, usually led by a band playing catchy music. The wagon also sported banners announcing when and where the circus would perform. As people followed the parade, their enthusiasm rose and some followers would even try to "get on the bandwagon." That phrase today still refers to the advertising approach that appeals to our need to be in step with everyone else.

Celebrity Endorsements

In this approach, the advertiser uses an "expert," such as an actor portraying a doctor who touts the excellence of a certain medicine to counteract our hay fever. Another tactic is to feature a favorite sports, music, or film celebrity who sings the praises of a product. Many people who endorse products promote them for positive reasons, but at times, endorsements are problematic. In the early nineties, Olympic figure skater Nancy Kerrigan complicated her endorsement deal with Disney when she was heard saying during a Disney parade: "This is so corny. This is so dumb. I hate it. This is the most corny thing I've ever done" (*Washington Post*). This celebrity endorsement approach can be very expensive for the advertiser because it often requires huge payoffs to the celebrity. The article "Nike Campaign Strikes at Firm's Record in Asia" (Inter-Press Agency) indicated that when basketball star Michael Jordan was advertising Nike shoes, the company paid Jordan more for his endorsement deal than it paid to its entire Indonesian workforce.

Exploiting Human Insecurity

There is a fine line between offering products that meet people's needs and taking advantage of human insecurity, which is another sales technique. This approach plays on our hidden fears of being physically offensive or of not measuring up in some way. The technique often is used to promote deodorants, for example, and it works! When feminine hygiene sprays were first introduced, women lined up to purchase them, convinced that they had been projecting terrible body odors for years. Unfortunately, the sprays at that time were actually dangerous to use.

The Image Transfer

The image transfer is another advertising technique. In this method, advertisers use one image to evoke another. Putting forth a slogan such as "Have your car smell like springtime" or using a duck to sell insurance are examples of this tactic. The image may have nothing to do with the item being sold, but it attracts attention and, advertisers hope, adds a compelling emotional resonance.

The "cute and sweet" approach utilizes puppies and babies to draw attention to products quite different than pet food and diapers. Similarly, a young woman in skimpy clothes often has nothing to do with the items she promotes, but her computer-enhanced image attracts viewers' eyeballs. Advertisers hope this attraction will lead to brand recognition.

Doublespeak

The doublespeak words used in ads may mean absolutely nothing other than a change of the container or the packaging. *New* and *improved* are examples of this form of advertising. In this age of multitasking, the *supersaver scheme* argues that a particular product will save you time and money or both. But if you listen closely to the narrative, the advertisers probably won you over at *supersaver* and, without lying outright, omitted an explanation of exactly what it is you will be saving or how much. *Easy* is another word that appeals to consumers, even though the product may not be easy to acquire, assemble, or even use.

Public Relations

An advertiser may also wish to simply raise a company's profile in the public eye—to improve its public image. Such an effort, whether in pursuit of media coverage or paid institutional promotion, is known as public relations, or "PR." In a media campaign, a company might issue press releases on company-related news, or make overtures to the press for fuller coverage. Strategies for paid institutional promotion might include advertorials—supplements in newspapers or magazines that look like feature stories but actually promote a particular product or service. The television counterpart to the advertorial is the infomercial: the advertiser pays to air a program that somewhat resembles a documentary about a product, service, or the institution as a whole.

Advertising Tobacco and Alcohol

Since their beginnings, tobacco and alcohol companies have promoted their products to underage consumers. Despite various warnings and laws from both health and government organizations, advertising to this audience remains a concern for parents, educators, health professionals, and young people themselves.

Tobacco

As early as 1929, American Tobacco spent $12.3 million to advertise its Lucky Strike cigarettes, the most any company had ever spent on single-product advertising up to that point. In 1964, after the U.S. surgeon general determined that "smoking is hazardous to your health," *The New Yorker* and other magazines banned cigarette ads. In 1971, Congress followed the surgeon general's lead and prohibited advertising of cigarettes on radio and television broadcasts. In 1998, cigarette makers and state attorneys general drafted a $206 billion deal that curbed tobacco marketing and settled lawsuits to compensate for tobacco-related Medicaid costs. The next year, the movie *The Insider* was released (1999, 157 minutes, rated R for language), including a now-famous scene in which tobacco executives testify that they did not know nicotine was addictive.

Alcohol

Alcohol is America's most widely used drug, legal for those age twenty-one and up.

In the 1890s, the first advertisements for alcohol (wines, liqueurs, and whiskeys) appeared in popular national magazines such as *Harper's Weekly*. A century later, the alcohol industry adopted voluntary advertising standards after a 1999 Federal Trade Commission recommendation suggested limiting alcohol promotion to underage consumers. Though they appear to be shielding young people from alcohol, these companies still spend millions upon millions of dollars placing ads where teens will see them.

A report in January 2006 titled "Youth Exposure to Alcohol Advertising in Magazines, 2001–2004: Good News, Bad News," published by the Center on Alcohol Marketing and Youth (CAMY) at Georgetown University, indicates that the alcohol industry is flooding youth-oriented magazines with ads, but the number of these ads decreased from 2001 to 2004. Though there was an overall decline, there are some very troubling statistics about alcohol advertising to Hispanic and African American youth, who seem to be targeted even more than their counterparts from other racial groups.

The Effects of Advertising Alcohol and Tobacco to Youth

The CAMY studies are troubling because we have known for a long time that alcohol contributes to the leading causes of death for youth: homicide, suicide, and unintentional injuries such as vehicle crashes and alcohol poisoning.

Evidence is growing that youth exposure to alcohol advertising plays a role in underage drinking. Once recent study followed young people over time in 24 media markets and found that for every additional alcohol ad they viewed over an average 23 per month, they drank 1% more. (L. B. Snyder et al., *Archives of Pediatrics and Adolescent Medicine* 160 (2006), pp. 18–24, cited in "Youth Exposure to Alcohol Advertising in Magazines," p. 2)

Another recent study used econometric analysis to estimate that a 28 percent decrease in youth exposure to alcohol advertising would result in a 4 to 16 percent drop in youth drinking and an 8 to 33 percent drop in youth binge drinking. (Saffer and Dave, in "Health Economics Early View" (13 February 2006), cited in "Youth Exposure to Alcohol Advertising in Magazines," p. 2)

The tobacco industry and alcoholic beverage companies provide education about the dangers of tobacco and alcohol respectively to youth, the same audience to whom they are trying to sell their products. Their advertising approach to youth lessens the companies' credibility as educators in prevention. The tobacco industry is at times required by the government to spend a certain amount on prevention education as part of legal settlements against big tobacco.

As long as youth are overloaded with social pressure and inundated with appealing ads selling them risky lifestyles, they—and their families and communities—will continue to pay a very high price.

Political Ads

Political advertising plays a significant role in the democratic process. Because politics is such a complex "business," campaign managers and lobbyists know that a media blitz shortly before election day is effective. Many citizens, either because of lack of critical thinking skills or busyness, rely on television and print ads to determine their vote.

Media mindfulness needs to be applied to political advertising. As we consider an ad for or against a candidate or ballot issue, we need to remember all the techniques advertisers use. When we approach political advertising in this manner, we can avoid the pitfalls of letting slick ads guide our vote.

The Church and Advertising

The Catholic Church has much to say about advertising. In its 1997 ecclesial pronouncement entitled *Ethics in Advertising*, the Vatican's Pontifical Council for Social Communications mentions the need for Catholic education about the role of advertising in today's world:

> We do not wish, and certainly we do not expect, to see advertising eliminated from the contemporary world. Advertising is an important element in today's society, especially in the functioning of a market economy, which is becoming more and more widespread.
>
> Moreover, for the reasons and in the ways sketched here, we believe advertising can, and often does, play a constructive role in economic growth, in the exchange of information and ideas, and in the fostering of solidarity among individuals and groups. Yet it also can do, and often does, grave harm to individuals and to the common good.
>
> In light of these reflections, therefore, we call upon advertising professionals and upon all those involved in the process of commissioning and disseminating advertising to eliminate its socially harmful aspects and observe high ethical standards in regard to truthfulness, human dignity and social responsibility. In this way, they will make a special and significant contribution to human progress and to the common good. (No. 23)

Characteristics of Some Advertising

- appeals to a target audience
- uses approaches that "sell" the product
- invites audiences to consider what they need and want
- is seductive
- uses clever phrases
- is often humorous
- can create artificial needs

Movies About Advertising

Use clips from these films to illustrate a point or begin a conversation, or show an entire film to your group and analyze it together.

What Women Want (2000, 127 minutes, rated PG-13). In this comedy, an advertising executive discovers he can read women's minds, learning their true thoughts about products on the market.

The Insider (1999, 157 minutes, rated R for language). The movie tells the story behind an episode of CBS's *60 Minutes* that investigated the wrongs of the U.S. tobacco industry. The segment was not aired at first because Westinghouse was negotiating the purchase of CBS at the time, and the network's lawyers thought this episode would interfere.

Bob Roberts (1992, 102 minutes, rated R: use selected scenes only). In this political satire, a folksinger runs a crooked election campaign to become a senator.

Things to Remember When Talking with Teens About Advertising

- Do not disparage advertising in general.
- Do point out the benefits of advertising.
- Do remind young people that they are a lucrative target audience.
- Do encourage them to use critical thinking skills when considering ads.

Media Saints and Greats

Saint Bernardine of Siena (1380–1444), an Italian Franciscan priest, used dramatic ways of preaching the word of God. Saint Bernardine also introduced the "IHS" symbol (the first three letters of Jesus's name in Greek, surrounded by rays), which is used by Holy Name Societies.

Saint John Bosco (1815–1888) was an Italian priest who founded the Salesian order. He used juggling and magic tricks to attract street youth so he could tell them Bible stories.

M edia Detective

Give these interesting and fun assignments to your students so they can investigate the media. Have them report back!

- Find out how much a thirty-second commercial during the Super Bowl will cost this season.
- Find several ways advertising is used by churches.
- Find out when the first political ad appeared in the United States.
- Find the name of the street in New York City that is often associated with the advertising industry.
- Find out what soft drink was first advertised in the United States.
- Find out what breakfast food was first mass-marketed in the United States.
- Find out how the Nielsen Media Research and Arbitron Radio Research ratings work.

- Do let them analyze the influence of advertising on adults.

Activities

Activity 1: Commercial Critics

In this activity, young people assess the effectiveness of advertisements that are directed at them.

1. Prepare for this activity by gathering commercials from current TV shows that are popular with teens. (You can ask the young people to tape commercials from some of their favorite shows and bring them to the session.)

2. Share the following information with the young people.

- ✦ The average American teen watches more than 20,000 TV commercials a year. American youth are a huge target demographic. Even if we claim that we don't pay attention

to commercial advertising, we have to realize that advertisers spend millions to discover what's "cool" with teens, and how to attract their attention, subtly or otherwise.

- ✦ These techniques and in-depth psychological studies fuel an ordinary TV commercial, especially those directed to youth. Shows popular with the youth culture are the place to showcase ads designed to "brand" the viewers.
- ✦ It is not just the ads that sell fashions, foods, attitudes and values, but the actual shows themselves. Whatever the genre of the show, stars wear hip clothes, flashy jewelry, and foot fashions that young people are enticed to buy.

3. Give a green card and a red card to each participant. Tell them to look at the commercial clips that you will show them, and to respond silently by holding up the green card if the commercial caught their attention and did a good job of promoting the product, or the red card not. After each clip, have someone make a tally. Ask those who raised green cards to tell the others why they did so. Then ask those who held up red cards to do the same.

4. Replay one commercial the youth found effective and one they thought was less effective. Ask the students to identify the reasons for the difference in appeal. Have students ask themselves whether they are more susceptible to certain advertising techniques than others.

Activity 2: "Jesus Ads" Competition

In this activity, students will plan an advertising campaign that respects human dignity.

1. Explain to the group that the Vatican Congregation, which promotes evangelization throughout the world, is called *Propaganda Fide* (Promotion of the Faith). Have the young people imagine that they are members of an advertising agency hired by *Propaganda Fide* to "pitch" Jesus to American teenagers.

2. Pair up the students. Then have each pair design a media campaign that respects human dignity. (You may want to have the students articulate some techniques that might honor or disrespect people's dignity.) They can use the Internet to identify the components of the campaign, including slogans, ads, product placement, giveaways, and so on, or if computers are not available, they can analyze newspaper ads, magazine ads, or direct mail pieces for ideas.

3. When each pair has designed its campaign, have them share it with the whole group, which will act as a focus group.

4. Ask students to vote for the campaign that seems the strongest. Have them list some of the reasons for its effectiveness. See if there is a way at least part of it can be implemented as part of a parish or school event.

Activity 3: Ads in Our Midst

In this activity, the young people look at various methods used by advertisers to sell products, and then identify instances of these techniques in action.

1. Prepare for this activity by assembling a few dozen magazines.

2. Begin the session by noting that we are surrounded by products of all kinds: in our backpacks, bathroom cabinets, refrigerators, and even on our heads and feet! These products and their promotion is what advertising is all about. They are also the focus of this activity.

3. Remind the group that the process of advertising itself is neither good nor bad. While advertising points out to us the many goods and services that are offered for our choice and purchase, many advertisers are skilled at convincing us that we need a particular good or service. The trick in consuming advertising is more than just choosing well—it is being aware of the various techniques that advertisers use so we can be mindful consumers.

4. Pass out copies of handout 3–A, "Advertising Techniques." Make the following points:

+ This handout has a sampling of the many devices that advertisers employ. They try to catch our attention just long enough to ensure product recall—that is, to guarantee that we remember the product and look for it when we shop.

+ Although there are many variations of these tactics, the ones listed are the most frequently utilized.

Review the handout with the young people. Invite brief reactions to, and examples of, the techniques they may have noticed.

5. Divide the group into teams of two or three, and display your supply of magazines. Ask each team to choose one or more techniques from the sheet; make sure all techniques are covered. Explain that the teams are to find ads in the magazines that best illustrate the use of their selected techniques. Suggest that the teams tear out the ads, analyze them, and hold them aside. Give the teams 10 to 15 minutes to search for the examples.

6. Then invite them together in the large group to explain and converse about what they discovered.

Activity 4: Media Mindfulness and Advertising

In this activity, the young people will use the four-step media mindfulness process to assess tobacco or alcohol ads.

1. Before the session, pick out several youth-oriented print ads for tobacco or alcohol. You might make overhead transparencies for easy viewing or create a PowerPoint presentation.

2. Pass out copies of handout 3–B, "Media Mindfulness and Advertising," and review the Advertising Mindfulness process, using the circle. Put an ad on an overhead or pass out copies. Have the students look at the ad and do their own personal

assessment of the ad, using the questions on the handout.

3. Then ask the students to share their analysis of the ad with those around them.

4. Finally, ask for input from the whole group, especially regarding the third and fourth steps of the media mindfulness strategy.

Reflective Exercise

Create a quiet environment. Play a meditation DVD with nature scenes and music to encourage the students to view it as an opportunity to thank God for God's self-disclosure in the gift of creation. Invite them to express inwardly the words or feelings that come as they watch and listen.

Closing Prayer

Jesus, you are the light of the world. Help us follow your light using the eyes of faith so that what we see in advertising will not turn us away from you but toward you. May we always realize that the things of earth will not be ours forever and that the good person is not the one who dies with the most toys. Amen.

Self-Evaluation

Please fill out a copy of appendix 6–A, "Self-Evaluation," in this manual.

Cross-Curricular Connections

Art. Analyze a color magazine ad using principles of graphic design: composition, color, typography, balance of text and images, and so on.

History. When a nation wages a war, it may well develop a public relations campaign associated with it. Look up such campaigns on the Ad Council Web site and debate their pros and cons.

Literature or Psychology. Read and critique Wakeman Frederic's classic *The Hucksters* (Rinehart and Company, 1946).

Advertising Techniques

Status Appeal

The strategy of status appeal touches the secret snob in us with slogans like "Be the first in your math class to sport Numb-Ear, the calculator earring!"

CELEBRITY ENDORSEMENT

The celebrity endorsement technique stresses that our favorite sports or media personalities use the product, with claims like "Tennis great Maria Love shaves her legs with Rip-Off; you can too!"

insecurity exploitation

The insecurity exploitation approach plays upon our hidden fears of being physically offensive or not measuring up in some way, with words like "Play it safe, use No Sweat deodorant spray."

IMAGE TRANSFER

The image transfer device employs one image to suggest another, with sentences like "Tournament cigarettes bring a winning taste to your mouth."

$UPER$AVER$

The supersavers scheme argues that a product will save you time or money, with slogans like "Car Brite works so fast it will give you time to clean your mom's car too!"

WORD TRAPS

The word traps ploy uses words that either mean nothing or are vague, with claims like "Zit-Go contains more of what most doctors recommend for trouble spots."

(This handout is from *Believing in a Media Culture*, by Gretchen Hailer, Thomas Zanzig, and Marilyn Kielbasa [Winona, MN: Saint Mary's Press, 1996], page 49. Copyright © 1996 by Saint Mary's Press. All rights reserved.

Media Mindfulness and Advertising

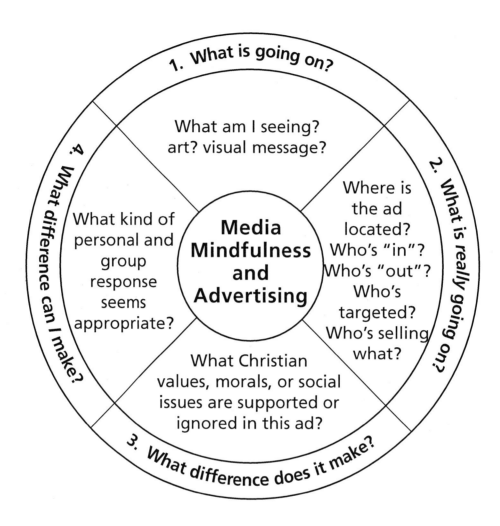

1. What is going on?

What am I seeing? art? visual message?

2. What is really going on?

Where is the ad located? Who's "in"? Who's "out"? Who's targeted? Who's selling what?

3. What difference does it make?

What Christian values, morals, or social issues are supported or ignored in this ad?

4. What difference can I make?

What kind of personal and group response seems appropriate?

Media Mindfulness and Advertising

(This diagram is adapted from *Believing in a Media Culture*, by Gretchen Hailer, Thomas Zanzig, and Marilyn Kielbasa [Winona, MN: Saint Mary's Press, 1996], page 38. Copyright © 1996 by Saint Mary's Press. All rights reserved.)

Chapter 4

Print and Media Mindfulness

Introduction

Scripture Connection

When he came to Nazareth, where he had been brought up, he went to the synagogue on the sabbath day, as was his custom. He stood up to read, and the scroll of the prophet Isaiah was given to him. He unrolled the scroll and found the place where it was written:

"The Spirit of the Lord is upon me,
   because he has anointed me
      to bring good news to the poor.
He has sent me to proclaim release to the captives
   and recovery of sight to the blind,
      to let the oppressed go free,
to proclaim the year of the Lord's favor."

And he rolled up the scroll, gave it back to the attendant, and sat down. The eyes of all in the synagogue were fixed on him. Then he began to say to them, "Today this scripture has been fulfilled in your hearing." (Luke 4:16–21)

In this Scripture passage, we see the vital connection between Jesus, the *Word* of God made flesh, and the *word* of God from the Hebrew writings. In his inaugural homily, we see Jesus perform the ministry of lector in his hometown community of Nazareth. When he receives the scroll from the attendant, he notices that the passage from the prophet Isaiah is about the very ministry to which he is called. Jesus reads about preaching the Reign of God to everyone. Through Baptism, we are incorporated into the life of God and contribute to God's Reign wherever we are and however we are uniquely called. For discerning believers, print media are more than just words, they are the means by which they can discover the Word made flesh and preach it as well.

Session Objectives

This session will enable you to accomplish the following tasks and goals:
- to assist young people in understanding the role of print media in our culture
- to help them explore the various genres of the print medium
- to give them a short history of the medium
- to orient them to a proper critique of print media
- to introduce them to the business of print publishing

- to help them consider the Church's attitude toward print media

---

What Are Print Media?

Print media consist of mechanically reproduced material disseminated in various formats, such as newspapers, books, pamphlets, and magazines.

The publishing industry generally values the following:

- stories
- clarity
- attractive design
- power
- influence
- mass audiences
- profit
- celebrities
- controversy
- sensationalism

Things to Know About Print Media

Print media embrace a number of genres, each playing a unique role in the world of communications. If we look back over the history of print publishing, we can see the origins of the print materials we use today.

Books

A Brief History of Books and Libraries in the United States

American school children used the first textbook, the *New England Primer*, from 1690 into the nineteenth century. This book taught the alphabet using religious texts. In the nineteenth century, the library system began in the United States. In 1800, the Library of Congress was established in Washington, D.C., by an act of Congress. By the middle of the century, Boston's public library was the first large, free, municipal library in the nation. The first edition of Webster's *American Dictionary of the English Language* appeared in 1828.

How Books Work

Books, like other print media, have many genres, generally categorized as either fiction or nonfiction. Fiction books are the product of the writer's imagination and are usually grouped into categories such as novel, mystery, romance, science fiction, fantasy, western, and so on. Nonfiction books, on the other hand, present their account or subject as fact, but may nevertheless reflect the author's own approach or beliefs about a subject. Nonfiction includes biography, history, encyclopedias and other reference books, textbooks, scientific papers, and the like.

Book publishers are in the business of developing books and acquiring them from authors. A book publisher that is developing a series on wildlife will approach experts on bears and moose and ask them to write a book of a certain type. Large publishers often work with book agents who advocate for a writer's book on their behalf. If a publisher accepts a manuscript, they have acquired it. First an editor looks at a manuscript and, in conversation with an author, assesses its structure to determine how the content would best be delivered to the reader. Then the editor looks more closely at writing quality. A copy editor polishes the text, and designers lay out the pages and the cover in a way that will enhance the content. After the book is proofread, it is printed and bound. In the meantime, the book is priced, marketed to customers, and publicized. (The new practice of "print on demand" lets publishers limit inventory and print books quickly.)

Comic Books and Graphic Novels

Many young readers favor the print genre of comic books or, more recently, "graphic novels." What's the difference? Comic books were originally short collections of comic strips reprinted from the newspaper. These pamphlets, oftentimes the reading material of childhood, still feature superheroes and other familiar cartoon characters. In fact, many comic-book superheroes have made their way into television series or to Hollywood and the big screen. Comic books feature perennial favorites like Disney characters, Warner cartoon personalities, and Superman, Spider-Man, X-Men and the like. Actually, some of the older comics have made their way into museum collections. *Manga*, a Japanese comic-book genre, is becoming very popular in North America. Some *manga* has been adapted into *anime*, a style of animation also from Japan.

Graphic novels, on the other hand, are book-length comics. They also contain comic-like drawings, panels, and text bubbles. But graphic novels deal more with everyday events and issues, often personal struggles, and not with superheroes. Harvey Pekar (the American Splendor series) and Will Eisner (the Contract with God series) are two artists who popularized the term "graphic novel" with their award-winning books.

What Is a Book's Voice?

Though readers may be familiar with the style or opinions of a given author, readers may not always realize that a publishing house also has a voice. The house has decided what types of books to publish and usually looks for authors who will write on the desired topics and will reflect the "voice" of the publisher—that is, not put forth ideas that contradict the publisher's mission or values. Savvy readers can form an impression of a publisher and come to expect a certain political, religious, or social perspective from it. One house might publish for a general readership, while another, such as a university press, might be very scholarly.

One group of books might be called political satire. These publishers do not hide their perspective in these books but rather openly ridicule those with different opinions using humor and mockery. It is important for young people to learn to read critically, to understand the difference between different genres of writing, and to critique what they are reading accordingly.

Newspapers

A Brief History of Newspapers in the United States

America's first newspaper, *Publick Occurrences Both Forreign and Domestick*, was printed in Boston in 1690. Benjamin Franklin later played a key role in publishing in the colonies. Franklin first began the *Pennsylvania Gazette* in 1728 and four years later he launched *Poor Richard's Almanack*, which ran until 1757. In this almanac, Ben Franklin used the pseudonym "Poor Richard," which gave the publication its name. The *Old Farmer's Almanac* began its annual publication in 1792 and continues today.

The first American daily, the *Pennsylvania Packet and General Advertiser*, appeared in Philadelphia in 1771. Alexander Hamilton was among the founders (1801) of the *New York Evening Post*, which, as the *New York Post*, is the oldest daily newspaper in the United States with an unbroken publishing history. The first African American newspaper, *The Freeman's Journal*, began publication in 1827, while the first Native American paper, *The Cherokee Phoenix*, began the following year. The invention of a mechanical typesetting device, the first rotary press, and the typewriter boosted newspaper publishing in the first half of the nineteenth century.

Horace Greeley, one of the best-known figures in American journalism, was proprietor and editor of the *New York Tribune* from its inception in 1841 until 1872. Around this time, the first "pictorial" weekly newspapers emerged, featuring extensive illustrations of events in the news, either as woodcut engravings made from correspondents' sketches or using a new invention— photography.

During the 1890s, other features of the modern newspaper began to appear: bold "banner" headlines, extensive use of images, "funny pages," and thorough coverage of organized sporting events.

The rise of yellow journalism—a flamboyant, sensationalist, and irresponsible approach to news reporting—also marks this era. William Randolph Hearst could truthfully boast that his newspapers manufactured the public clamor for war on Spain in 1898.

Fifteen years later, most of the essential features of the modern newspaper had emerged. In 1913, the *New York World* printed the first crossword puzzle, still a favorite feature for many.

In the troubled 1960s and 1970s, the phenomenon of the "underground" or alternative press appeared throughout the country between 1965 and 1971. With names like *Free Press*, *Rising Up Angry*, and *Student Mobilizer*, these short communiqués allowed people to speak out against issues such as war, racism, and sexism.

In our time, radio, television, and the Internet have gradually supplanted newspapers as the nation's primary information sources. But newspaper journalism continues to play an important communication role, despite declining readership. At present, the top twenty newspaper publishing companies control more than 60 percent of the market.

How Newspapers Work

Newspapers have evolved in both form and content over the years, now appearing on the Internet as well in parallel electronic form. But the word *newspaper* still says what it is. It is a print vehicle that disseminates news. But of course, there is the obvious question: What is news? News seems rather hard to define, but it can be described as something out of the ordinary, abnormal—something new. The news industry reports on current events, pointing to both human failure and success. Newspapers inform the reader about world, national, and local happenings. Papers influence public opinion and policy through investigative reporting as well as editorial comment. They entertain us with human interest stories and features. And they also provide a means for businesses to advertise their products and services.

There are all kinds of newspapers, each serving a particular type of audience. *USA Today* is the national daily with the largest circulation and readership in the United States. The *Los Angeles Times*, the *New York Times*, the *Washington Post*, and the *Times-Picayune* of New Orleans are examples of metropolitan dailies.

There are about two thousand newspaper publishing companies in the United States, bringing in annual revenue of $50 billion for a combined circulation of slightly less than sixty million readers. A variety of special-interest papers serve readerships such as various ethnic groups and speakers of other languages. There are also "tabloids," papers printed in a half-size format. While some "supermarket tabloids" such as the *National Enquirer* or *Weekly World News* tend to print sensationalized stories, bizarre features, and celebrity profiles, many people read them as they would an ordinary newspaper, thinking (or perhaps, choosing to believe) that they are reading actual facts. Many famous personalities, concerned about their reputations and the safety of their families, have sued these papers or pursued court orders to keep these photographers—also called the paparazzi—and reporters away from them.

Some religious publications also take the form of newspapers. The *National Catholic Reporter* is a forum for Church-related issues. Various diocesan communications (newspapers and Web sites) usually report more extensively on diocesan events and activities.

The Newspaper Business

One of the reasons we see so much advertising in newspapers is that newspapers are businesses whose bottom line is revenue. Advertising dollars typically represent 70 percent of a paper's revenue. If the ads did not exist, neither would the newspaper!

An ordinary daily paper has a publisher who acts as CEO, but the person who really runs the paper is the editor-in-chief. If the paper is large, he or she is assisted by a number of section editors. Reporters and photographers answer to these editors, who usually assign them to the various stories that need to be covered that day. Once written, each article is turned over to a copy editor, who checks the facts, grammar, and spelling, and then hands it over to a headline editor. He or she writes a catchy headline to draw attention to the story. Finally, it is sent to the graphics department for layout. From here, the files are sent to press. Once the edition is printed, the circulation department ensures that the finished paper is delivered on time to subscribers, newsstands, and other outlets.

Newspaper journalists are careful most of the time to write in a way that is in keeping with the perspective and values of a given newspaper. It would be a mistake to think that every article is an objective presentation of the truth. Every decision newspaper managers make reflects their values: who they hire, what they cover, what they cut, and so on. This may be more obvious at election time when many newspapers endorse candidates, but it is important to remember every time we pick up the paper. Newspapers include material that reflects their belief system or that will make them money. If we believe that what is in the paper is "the way the world is," then we will easily become discouraged, as tragedy and bad news sell more papers than good news.

News Stories

Now what about the news stories themselves? Usually they are divided into topical sections, with the biggest story, called the lead story, appearing on page one, usually on the top right corner to catch our attention. In addition to the straight news sections, most papers have extra sections for sports, entertainment (puzzles, horoscope, comics, and so on), health, business, and culture. Newspapers also run editorials that reflect the worldview of these "media gatekeepers" of public opinion. These columns, often unsigned, comment on international, national, or local events.

Reporters generally follow a time-honored approach, using the "5 Ws and an H" to cover their material: Who? What? Where? When? Why? and How? The opening paragraph of a story is called the lead; writers try to cover these questions briefly there. Writers use a formula called an inverted pyramid, placing the most salient facts first, and the rest in descending order of importance. Then, if a copy editor has to cut some of the story, the essentials have already appeared in the lead.

Some articles and photos may come from syndicated sources such as Associated Press, Reuters, or Catholic News Service: agencies that sell news material to subscriber papers around the world.

Magazines

Magazines provide readers with information about all kinds of topics. There are about 18,250 magazine titles available in the United States. Whereas newspapers, radio, and television are considered mass media, print magazines are referred to as niche media because they usually aim at a very specific audience.

How Magazines Work

With the exception of news magazines like *Time* and *Newsweek*, magazines' focus is very specific. Usually their titles—such as *Motor Trends, Working Woman, House and Garden, Health and Fitness, Modern Photography, Entertainment Weekly*—let the reader know what kind of articles they will find inside. The ads inside will target the magazine's largest reader demographic.

Some magazines or periodicals are called journals and are often connected with a professional, academic, or other field. For example, the *New England Journal of Medicine,* a serious periodical about current medical research, is not only read by physicians but is often quoted on radio, television, and in newspapers.

Niche Magazines

Recently, some of the most popular sports, entertainment, and fashion magazines have launched parallel issues for teens. The marketing strategy for these publications is simple. The companies that produce the magazines want to reach out early and "brand" young readers, claiming their loyalty to the particular title (as well as the products advertised) as they mature. Many of these magazines targeted for teens contain endless stories, gossip really, about celebrities, recounting who is dating whom, which couple has broken up, and who has been through a rehab facility. Such stories appeal to readers' curiosity about high-profile people, but unfortunately they tend also to normalize the behavior reported in them. This behavior is rarely in keeping with the family or religious values of mainstream America.

These magazines, like newspapers, are heavily subsidized by advertising. And, of course, with full-color ads, the marketers can create slick ad campaigns to promote products for a niche readership. Clothing, cosmetics, cell phones, iPods, fast foods—all the pop-culture paraphernalia that convey "cool"—are the subjects of these ads.

We choose particular magazines for different purposes. We may want to be entertained or learn something new or try to figure out what is happening in the world. The critical reader learns where the most reliable information can be found. A fashion magazine is more likely than a news magazine to tell me what I should wear to be fashionable. If I look to learn about a political candidate in the fashion magazine, however, it may give me a story on the candidate's family and former life but will less likely inform me about his or her stand on important issues. Some diocesan publications present the Catholic stance on election issues and could help me discern which candidate shares Catholic values.

Movies About Print Media

Use clips from these films to illustrate a point or begin a conversation, or show an entire film to your group and analyze it together.

Absence of Malice (1981, 116 minutes, rated PG). A reporter inadvertently ruins the life of a warehouse owner by publishing a leaked story in which all the facts are accurate—but nothing is true.

You've Got Mail (1998, 118 minutes, rated PG). A man and woman begin an anonymous online relationship without realizing they are rivals in real life: he wants to buy the land where her little bookstore is located.

Spider-Man 2 (2004, 127 minutes, rated PG-13). In this sequel, newspaperman Spider-Man Peter Parker must recognize and follow his true calling, a move that requires great virtue and means that he cannot simply choose the life of a newspaper photographer.

The Church and Print Media

Johann Gutenberg invented movable type and the prototype of the printing press in about 1455. The first book he mass produced was a Bible. A few years later, the Protestant Reformation began, and the Catholic Church began to censor what could be printed, sold, and read by the laity. The first Roman Index or *List of Prohibited Books* (*Index Librorum Prohibitorum*) was published by Pope Paul IV in 1557, and was added to continually over the centuries.

Since Vatican Council II, the Catholic Church has been less strict about print media than in the past, and the decision was made, by Pope Paul VI in 1966, to retire the practice of adding books to the Index. The original document itself, however, has never been repealed.

At this time, Canon Law requires that any book about Catholic faith and morals receive an *imprimatur*—meaning "it may be printed"—from the bishop of the place where an author resides or the publisher is located.

The Catholic Church is concerned about pornography of all kinds, including print, and its effects on those who produce it and those who read it. In 1989, the Vatican issued a document, *Pornography and Violence in the Communications Media: A Pastoral Response,* that reinforces what research has proven: no one is immune from the effects of pornography, and young people are especially vulnerable. (See chapter 9 of this book for more on pornography in general, and on the Church's teaching about it.)

Characteristics of the Print Media Industry

- creates a mass audience
- encourages reading
- is an important element of a democracy
- requires significant environmental resources
- provides information and entertainment

Media Saints and Greats

Saint Francis de Sales (1567–1622), a Swiss priest, was renowned for writing simple explanations of doctrine and spirituality. He also was a prolific correspondent.

Blessed Titus Brandsma (1881–1942) was a Dutch Carmelite priest, translator, author, journalist, and newspaper editor. He was executed in a Nazi concentration camp for criticizing Nazi propaganda and policies.

Flannery O'Connor (1925–1964) was an American novelist from the South. Her writings often revealed Christ and redemption in unusual people and places.

Media Detective

Give these interesting and fun assignments to your students so they can investigate the media. Have them report back!

- Find the top five daily newspapers in the United States, based on circulation figures.
- Identify a country that is very risky for foreign journalists.
- Find the graphic novel that won a Pulitzer Prize.
- Find three magazines for adults that that also have teen versions.
- Find the most recent winner of the National Magazine Award for best Internet news source.
- Find out the name of the oldest Catholic newspaper in the United States and the oldest one in Canada.
- Find some books in classic literature that are on the *List of Forbidden Books.*
- Find the awards given to Catholic publications, and to interfaith periodicals.
- Find out the name of the award given to comic book designers.
- Find out the seven things Catholics can do to respond to the problems of pornography and violence. (Direct them to the 1989 document *Pornography and Violence in the Communications Media.*)

Things to Remember When Talking with Teens About Print Media

- Do encourage them to read widely.
- Do not belittle their preferred print genres.
- Do challenge them to read the classics.
- Do not embarrass poor readers by having them read aloud.
- Do give extra help to struggling readers.
- Do caution them about pornography.

Activities

Activity 1: Front Page Search

In this activity, the students search the front pages of newspapers for evidence of gender bias.

1. In preparation for this activity, collect the front pages of newspapers over several weeks, one for each young person. (Do not give students the entire newspaper; it may distract them.) Use national and local papers and at least one local Catholic newspaper.

2. Give each student two markers of different colors. Instruct them to read the entire front page and circle in one color all the female first names and pronouns they see, including the names of reporters and photographers, and faces in photos. With the second color, they should circle all the male names, pronouns, and faces in photos. (If they cannot differentiate the sex of the person, they should just skip the name or photo.) If they find words that always refer to a male or female—for example, a nun— or a known official, they should circle those too.

3. When the students have finished, ask them to count the male and female circles they made, then calculate the ratio by dividing the larger number by the smaller. For example, 55 males to 5 females creates a ratio of 11 to 1.

4. Have the students hold up their circled front pages so that everyone can get a visual idea of others' findings.

5. Ask each student to state his or her ratio and talk about the results and what they might mean. Ask the class: Who does the front page seem to consider important?

Activity 2: Create a New Magazine

In this activity, the young people engage their creativity and understanding of print media and human dignity to design and launch a new magazine.

1. Introduce the activity by telling the students that they will be starting a new magazine. They can create a magazine for any niche audience they believe will be interested in it—and the magazine's contents must respect human dignity.

2. Collect a few dozen magazine titles and make them available for the students to consult. Pass out copies of handout 4–A, "Designing a New Magazine Worksheet."

3. Divide the students into groups of three. Have each group work together to decide on elements of for their magazine such as a title, general style and tone, cover graphics, page format, permanent sections, editorial point of view, positioning of ads, and so on. (Encourage each small group to poll fellow classmates for content suggestions for their magazine.) Remind the students to determine the frequency of the publication as well as the cover price.

4. Ask each group to prepare a mock-up of the first issue and then be prepared to present its new publication to the other groups.

5. Poll the other students to see how many would actually buy such a magazine. Or, if the subject matter is not to their taste, ask the other young people how attractive they believe the magazine would be to the niche audience.

Activity 3: Popcorn, Prayer, and a Movie

In this activity, the young people analyze and critique a movie from the perspective of media ethics, and practice the art of respectful dialogue.

Plan a movie night for viewing one of the films listed in this chapter, or another movie of your choice. Preview the movie and create some follow-up questions for conversation and reflection with your students. For example, if you choose *Absence of Malice*, talk about journalistic ethics (the right to print the truth and the public's right to know), as

Cross-Curricular Connections

 Literature. Have the students read a short story from a magazine, then either edit it or write and report on it.

Social Studies or Geography. Find several issues of *Maryknoll* magazine and discuss the lives of overseas missionaries.

Science or Technology. Research the evolution of print from Gutenberg to books-on-demand and e-books.

well as the morality of revenge. Ask, Does the truth always set everyone free?

If the tone of the evening seems appropriate, set aside some time at the end to pray for reporters who have lost their lives while doing their jobs.

Activity 4: Print and Media Mindfulness

The purpose of this activity is to apply the media mindfulness strategy to any type of print media.

Reflective Exercise

Create a quiet setting. Pass out pages of the daily newspaper to all the students. Play some quiet instrumental music. Ask the students to read the page they have received and to formulate a short prayer based on something found there. Then begin a litany similar to the Prayers of the Faithful at Mass, to which each contributes his or her prayer. Ask the group to respond with some phrase such as "God, hear our prayerful words."

Closing Prayer

Eternal God, you sent your Son Jesus into this world as your *Word* made flesh. Help us to heed Jesus's words about you that we read in the four Gospels. And be with us to spread the Good Word to others. Amen.

Self-Evaluation

Please fill out a copy of appendix 6–A, "Self-Evaluation," in this manual.

Designing a New Magazine Worksheet

Magazine Element	Our Magazine	✔
Target Audience		
Name		
Format (size of magazine, cover, page design)		
Number of Pages		
Editorial Point of View		
Permanent Sections 1. 2. 3. 4. 5. 6. 7.		
Advertising – what kind		
How will the magazine be marketed?		

Media Mindfulness and Print

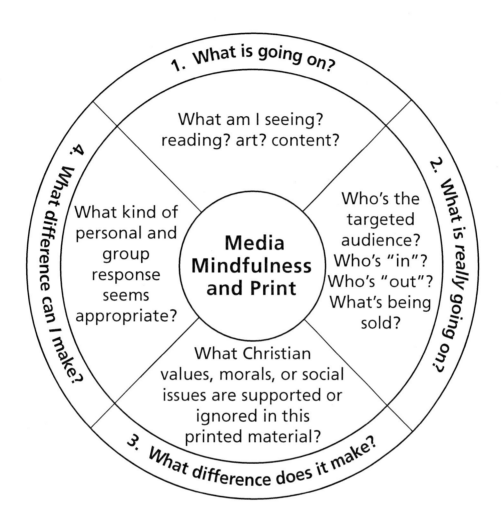

1. **What is going on?**

What am I seeing? reading? art? content?

2. **What is really going on?**

Who's the targeted audience? Who's "in"? Who's "out"? What's being sold?

3. **What difference does it make?**

What Christian values, morals, or social issues are supported or ignored in this printed material?

4. **What difference can I make?**

What kind of personal and group response seems appropriate?

Media Mindfulness and Print

(This diagram is adapted from *Believing in a Media Culture,* by Gretchen Hailer, Thomas Zanzig, and Marilyn Kielbasa [Winona, MN: Saint Mary's Press, 1996], page 38. Copyright © 1996 by Saint Mary's Press. All rights reserved.)

Chapter 5

Movies and Media Mindfulness

Introduction

Scripture Connection

> Then the disciples came and asked him, "Why do you speak to them in parables?" He answered, "To you it has been given to know the secrets of the kingdom of heaven, but to them it has not been given. For to those who have, more will be given, and they will have an abundance; but from those who have nothing, even what they have will be taken away. The reason I speak to them in parables is that 'seeing they do not perceive, and hearing they do not listen, nor do they understand.'" (Matt. 13:10–13)

In this passage, the disciples ask Jesus why he speaks to the crowds through parables. He tells them that people best understand the Good News through the use of stories that draw people to ponder the deeper meaning of life. Later, in this same chapter from Matthew, Jesus compares the Reign of God to many things and situations familiar to the people so that they understand his message. The disciples are blessed because they know Jesus personally. Their eyes see and their ears hear Jesus's message of love.

Some stories told through movies are like parables and contain "seeds of the Gospel" that lead us to deeper, transcendent meaning. If we take the time to view deeply and listen carefully, we will see beyond the obvious to discover what the movie means and how God might be teaching us through it.

Session Objectives

This session will enable you to accomplish the following tasks and goals:
- to explore with young people how movies entertain and inform
- to help them understand movie-making as a business
- to show them how and why worldviews and ideologies are embedded in movies
- to help them appreciate film as an art and a storytelling medium
- to help them notice "seeds of the Gospel" present in the movies
- to acquaint them with the Church's attitude toward movies
- to teach them how to critique a film

What Is a Movie?

The movie medium informs or entertains us by telling a story through a moving sequence of celluloid or digital photographic scenes. Movies are also called films, motion pictures, and cinema.

The movie industry generally values the following.
* good storytelling
* entertainment
* the cult of celebrity
* special techniques and effects
* attracting attention
* commercialization and consumerism
* creativity and art
* exploitation of the human body to gain an audience

Things to Know About Movies

Movies have been a significant part of mass media culture for more than a century. Movies entertain us in theaters and, today, in our homes through DVDs, pay-per-view, network, cable, and satellite television, as well as via the Internet.

Movies are a multi-billion-dollar industry in the United States. Although India's Hindi film industry, informally called "Bollywood," produces more films than does the United States every year, no other country's output comes near that of the Unites States in terms of economic profit or global cultural influence—the latter a contentious issue between the United States and many countries.

A Brief History of the Movies in the United States

Technologies developed in the nineteenth century —photography, electricity, electric light—converged with ingenuity to inspire the creation of motion pictures. Movies "work" when a series of visual frames pass by at the rate of twenty-four per second, the brain recalls a scene that the next scene will build upon. As a mode of storytelling, film can deal with fiction (features) or nonfiction (documentaries); or it can blend those genres. Film language—its true storytelling power—began in 1900 when film editing was introduced. (Before that, a single sequence of real-time footage was shot.) This technique allowed the filmmaker to craft a story according to a genre and to market the film to both specific and broad markets.

A mass audience for films soon grew. Movies, even silent ones—the first talking film was released in 1927—were hugely entertaining, and Americans spent increasing amounts of disposable income going to the movies. Movies now draw people to build DVD libraries.

The film business in the United States gained its powerful edge early on and has maintained its cultural and economic dominance for two principal reasons: World War I and the European view that cinema is primarily an art form.

European countries were already making significant contributions to cinema before World War I. But their filmmaking was disrupted by the war, which devastated the economic and cultural infrastructures of these countries. Meanwhile, in the United States, fledgling filmmakers moved from the New York–New Jersey area to southern California, where the climate allowed for year-round location shooting, helping the business to prosper and develop into the studio system.

The American view of film as business and as entertainment fueled the booming industry in the United States, whereas the understanding of film as art continues to color the way Europeans produce and understand films. Since the Renaissance in the fourteenth and fifteenth centuries, Europe's wealthy people, and even its governments, have been patrons of the arts. Modern European governments have also always supported the work of filmmakers with less regard for distribution and economic success.

A new advancement in cinema, digital filmmaking is now beginning to replace conventional

35 millimeter methods. George Lucas is a pioneer in this field: he shot almost all of *Star Wars Episode II: Attack of the Clones* using digital means.

Digital filmmaking is cost effective because the equipment is less expensive; indeed, it broadens the art form's accessibility. The digital images in binary data are nonlinear and can be edited on a computer, rather than in thousands of feet of actual film. The switch from traditional to digital filmmaking will entail a major shift in how movies are produced and who produces them. Many film aficionados think that digital films are not films at all because they provide a different experience, a different "feel" for moviegoers. These critics fear that the texture of the film will not evoke the same emotional response from audiences.

How Filmmaking Works

All filmmakers use techniques to craft their stories, to convey ideas and to evoke an emotional response that keeps audiences coming back for more. Camera techniques include movement (such as panning), careful framing and deliberate camera angles, establishing shots, medium shots, and close-ups. Close-up shots in particular create an intimate relationship between a screen character and the audience, because they lead us to care about the character. Who and what will be in the frame, and how important these elements are at that moment, determine how a shot is framed. Filmmakers also use techniques such as lighting, colors, set designs, and costumes to achieve what they desire.

Filmmakers generate special effects (F/X) by adding computer-generated effects to edited film. These effects can enhance the storytelling and the audience's visual experience. Computer-generated images (CGIs) may even be used to populate the film instead of actors. These techniques were used frequently in the Star Wars prequel series (1999, 2002, and 2005), the Lord of the Rings trilogy (2001, 2002, and 2003), and *The Chronicles of Narnia: The Lion, the Witch and the Wardrobe* (2005).

Sound has great emotional power. Music and sound effects cue us to what is about to happen and how we should feel about it. Music is physical because sound works by vibrating our eardrums. When music is mixed well with visuals, we may either sit on the edge of our seats, scream, cry, or laugh. Some sound effects have become clichés, such as storms that signal that something is going to change in the story, usually for the worse. Coughing by a main character may signal future sickness or possibly death. A train crossing is often a symbol for making a decision. Visual motifs, such as water scenes, can add depth to our interpretation, while stock action sequences, such as car chases, add thrills.

Worldview and the Cinema

All films reflect the worldviews of the filmmaker and his or her collaborators—the writer(s), cinematographers, and soundtrack and music composers. Philosophic, religious, political, and economic ideologies may be embedded in the stories. Many films reflect the political status quo of their country of origin, because it is that political system that permits the filmmaker to exist and work. When films *do* challenge the political status quo in the United States, however, they can be decried as unpatriotic—even if the filmmaker is only expressing his or her First Amendment rights.

Human experience affects what films are made and how they are interpreted. The filmmaker has a story to tell and it is shaped by his or her own life experience; human, moral, and faith development; professional training; family life; and education. Media mindfulness teaches that there is no right or wrong way to interpret a film. We may see the same film (or hear the same homily) and understand them very differently because we see and interpret films through the lenses of our own experiences, education, and faith formation as well. The important thing is that we listen to one another's opinions with respect, and that we always seek to further develop our critical skills.

Films are rated by the sensibilities of the culture into which they are released. This is why a film like *Dead Man Walking* (1995, 122 minutes) may get an R rating in the United States, but a PG in Singapore, and an under-fifteen restriction in the United Kingdom. Sensibilities can change over time as well. People may not get as upset over a controversial film ten years after it is released. Often the promotion of a film creates more sensation than the film itself delivers—once people actually *see it.*

It is important to assess what worldview is expressed in a film. Those involved in the production of *Saved!* (2004, 92 minutes, rated PG-13) put forth a religious ideology that questions the status quo of a Christian high school. *The Exorcism of Emily Rose* (2005, 119 minutes, rated PG-13) is about a Catholic exorcism ritual, but still, interestingly, the underlying theological ideology sounds Calvinist, that is, implying that human beings have little or no free will but rather their fate is predetermined for them by God. All Disney movies have happy endings and their marketers try to convince us that buying products connected to the film, such as toys, clothing, bedding, and soundtracks will make us feel even better.

A film's use of negative stereotypes about women, the elderly, people from different cultures, and social class can tell us something about the producer's worldview. A way to identify a film's secular ideology, for example, is to recognize that the movie uncritically accepts as normal behaviors that are contrary to Christian morality. Such behaviors include engaging in sex before, or outside, of marriage; artificial contraception; abortion; adultery; drug, alcohol, and tobacco abuse; and lack of civility due to gratuitous offensive language and violence presented as mainstream entertainment. Many films have a wordview reflecting postmodernism, an ideology that is detached from an understanding of history or any idea of objective right or wrong.

A film will meet our expectations as Christians and be an enjoyable experience if, by the end, it resolves the dramatic or comedic conflict in ways that respect human dignity. The best films actually do this. In order to show redemption, however, it is often necessary to also show the sin so we sufficiently understand the conflict.

Movie Rating Systems

In 1922, a film review board called the Motion Picture Producers and Distributors of America (MPPDA) was established in Hollywood to censor films. The public had begun to fear that the immorality associated with some celebrities would appear in the films in which they starred. Will H. Hays, the former postmaster general of the United States, was the head of the board. In 1930, the film industry adopted the famous Production Code (also known as the Hays Code) in hopes that the many censorship groups that had sprung up around the country would follow one code to determine a film's morality. In 1934, the MPPDA began enforcing the code.

Though restrictive, almost every Hollywood filmmaker adhered to the rules of the Hays Code. It regulated topics such as violence, the treatment of religion, and how long a film kiss could last and said that "the treatment of bedrooms must be governed by good taste and delicacy" (ArtsReformation.com Web site)—which was interpreted to mean that twin beds would appear on the set.

The biggest problem with the Hays Code was interpreting what terms like *indecent, ridicule, correct entertainment*, and eventually *pornography* actually meant. But the Hays Code remained in effect until it was replaced in 1967 with the Motion Picture Code and Rating Program. The former MPDAA became the Motion Picture Association of America (MPAA), which now rates rather than censors movies.

The National Legion of Decency was founded in the United States in April 1934 to combat immoral films and to boycott any film that did not adhere to the Hays Code. Parishioners pledged in church to avoid bad films.

After Vatican II, the Church in the United States began to take a more positive approach to cinema, leaving behind a language of censorship and redefining its role as providing information for guidance. The Office for Film and Broadcast (OFB) was established in 1966 and initiated its own rating system.

Most ratings are largely based on content analysis—that is, a counting of how many obscenities, acts of violence or sexuality, and episodes of alcohol and drug use appear in the film. Taking these behaviors out of the story's context can suggest to audiences that they should focus only on the negative elements of the film—whereas the movie as a whole might truly tell a story of redemption and grace.

Ratings can help parents who seek guidance about what is age-appropriate for their children to see. Ratings do not absolve parents or guardians, however, from explaining to children the reasons to avoid a certain film. This type of communication is the only way parents can pass their values about movies on to their children.

The Church and Movies

The first official Church document to address modern communications other than print was the encyclical letter *On Motion Pictures* (*Vigilanti Cura*), written in 1936 by Pope Pius XI. The second was *On Motion Pictures, Radio, and Television* (*Miranda Prorsus*), issued in 1957 by Pope Pius XII. The most significant document to be written is the *Decree on the Media of Social Communications* (*Inter Mirifica*) from the Second Vatican Council in 1963.

On Motion Pictures, the 1936 document, was concerned specifically with the way cinema then portrayed sin and vice, and it praised the foundation of the National Legion of Decency. The document recommended that each nation establish a central office to review, rate, and even censor movies. You can see elements of 1940s Church censorship at the time in the film *Cinema Paradiso* (1989, 155 minutes, rated R).

Though the Pope said positive things about the cinema in *On Motion Pictures, Radio, and Television* (*Miranda Prorsus*), he viewed movies with caution:

> Just as very great advantages can arise from the wonderful advances which have been made in our day, in technical knowledge concerning Motion Pictures, Radio and Television, so too can very great dangers.

Although the *Decree on the Media of Social Communications* (*Inter Mirifica*) embraces all mass media, audiences, and producers in its scope, the two paragraphs applied to movies possess a similar caution. The Vatican document also includes some suggestions to Catholics about making the most of this medium:

> The production and showing of films that have value as decent entertainment, humane culture or art, especially when they are designed for young people, ought to be encouraged and assured by every effective means. This can be done particularly by supporting and joining in projects and enterprises for the production and distribution of decent films, by encouraging worthwhile films through critical approval and awards, by patronizing or jointly sponsoring theaters operated by Catholic and responsible managers. (No. 14)

Vatican Council II opened up new ways for the Church to relate to modern media and to the People of God by demonstrating a keener awareness of how audiences use and make meaning from cinema. It implicitly acknowledges that people can use their own critical abilities to choose and judge films. In addition, Vatican II encourages lay involvement in media production and an approach resembling media mindfulness.

Pornography

Pornography in print, on the Internet, in adult theaters, and in DVDs is pervasive and easily available. Pornography debases and disrupts our relationships with each other and with God, especially when it is connected to violence. Soft porn is defined as the imitation of sexual intercourse, while in hardcore pornography, actual intercourse takes place. An indicator of a pornographic film is a focus on body parts and functions rather than the person as a whole—body, mind, and spirit. Because of the sexual arousal that pornography can stimulate in the person consuming it, porn is highly addictive. In 1989, the Pontifical Council for Social Communications defined the term in *Pornography and Violence in the Communications Media: A Pastoral Response:*

> Pornography in the media is understood as a violation, through the use of audio-visual techniques, of the right to privacy of the human body in its male or female nature, a violation which reduces the human person and human body to an anonymous object of misuse for the purpose of gratifying concupiscence; violence in the media may be understood—especially in this context—as a presentation designed to appeal to base human instincts or actions contrary to the dignity of the person and depicting intense physical force exercised in a deeply offensive and often passionate manner. (No. 9)

> Pornography and sadistic violence debase sexuality, corrode human relationships, exploit individuals—especially women and young people—undermine marriage and family life, foster anti-social behaviour and weaken the moral fibre of society itself. (No. 10)

> Thus, one of the clear effects of pornography is sin. (No. 11)

Characteristics of Movies

- tell stories with a great sense of realism
- use sound and image to create meaning
- are a popular form of entertainment
- can inspire social and cultural change
- convey the filmmaker's worldview or ideology

Movies About Film

Use clips from these films to illustrate a point or begin a conversation, or show an entire film to your group and analyze it together.

Cinema Paradiso (1989, 155 minutes, rated R). Despite the film's rating, the opening sequences of the film are suitable for teens and provide a historical glimpse of the Church's relationship with cinema.

Singin' in the Rain (1952, 103 minutes, rated G). This classic is a look at Hollywood's musicals and a spoof on the transition from silent films to "talkies."

Guilty by Suspicion (1991, 105 minutes, rated PG-13). A film director is called before the House Committee on Un-American Activities during the 1950s Hollywood Blacklist era and refuses to name names to those hunting communists in America.

S1mOne (2002, 117 minutes, rated PG-13). A washed-up director creates a virtual movie star on a computer, devises a simulated life for her, and makes her a celebrity who everyone thinks is real.

- are expensive to make; moderately expensive to see
- constitute a big business in the United States
- are a revered art form in many other countries

Things to Remember When Talking with Teens About Movies

- Do analyze, judge, and speak about only those movies you have actually seen.
- Do remember that there is no right or wrong way to *interpret* movies.
- Do be open to the different understandings young people have regarding movies.
- Do find out a film's rating, and what various critics are saying about the movie.

- Do remember that an R rating does not mean a film is bad; it often means that the material requires the wisdom and guidance of an adult.
- Do be aware of what teens are going to see and be sure you see it too so you can speak to the film with credibility. There are some R-rated films that many teens see.
- Do remember that there is more to a film than the sex, bad language, and violence it may contain: consider the context, the story, and how the plot is resolved.

Media Detective

Give these interesting and fun assignments to your students so that they can "investigate" the media. Have them report back!

- Find out who invented and developed the early cinema, when, and in what countries.
- Find out what genres of movies exist, define them, and find one or two examples that illustrate each.
- Find out the major differences between traditional celluloid filmmaking and digital filmmaking.
- Find out the title of the first talking movie.
- Find out how filmmaking today differs from the studio system of the first sixty years of cinema in the United States.
- Find out what independent film is.
- Find out who was Russia's most famous pre–World War I filmmaker and the titles of some of his films.
- Find out who the current top three female directors in the United States are.
- Find out why countries rate films differently.
- Find out how many official church statements (encyclicals, constitutions, apostolic letters, and documents) have been issued since the 1930's on cinema and other means of communication.
- Find out about the various awards for movie excellence.

- Do be assured that by talking about movies that do not reflect human and Gospel values in every way, we are not necessarily endorsing them.
- Do remember what it was like to be a teenager. Put yourself in the shoes of the young people with whom you share faith. Ask yourself, How old was I when my faith made a difference in the movies I chose to see, and once chosen, how did I analyze and think about what they meant to me?

Activities

Activity 1: Youth Film Festival

In this activity, the young people design a film festival.

These "Ten Steps for Planning a Youth Film Festival" provide you with all you need. Plan this festival with young people and delegate appropriate responsibilities to them.

1. Select a theme based on the festival's objective.

2. Create a budget.

3. Select a few age-appropriate films and preview them; make final choices and note the motivations for choosing each one.

4. Obtain a license for a public performance from Christian Video Licensing International (CVLI). A license is needed when showing a film outside a scheduled curriculum; check the lists of studios on the CVLI Web site to make sure the films you choose are covered by its license. (See appendix 4, "Fair Use of Media.")

5. Choose a date and screening times. Secure necessary permissions. Arrange for extra adults to be present if needed. Decide on the schedule.

6. Invite an expert (local newspaper film critic, college professor, actor) to converse about the film afterward, or choose someone to lead an audience conversation.

7. Identify the best space and reserve it. (Use a room that can be darkened.)

8. Prepare publicity such as posters, flyers, and a parish bulletin announcement (title of festival, theme, sponsoring organization, purpose, film schedule, list of invited professionals, and so on). Make sure parents are informed and invited.

9. Prepare a program for distribution at the event with more information about the theme, films, questions to reflect on, and so on.

10. Set up and check out all the equipment ahead of time (LCD projector or DVD player and monitor, screen, sound, room lighting, microphone if needed); set up the space, arrange for refreshments after the screening.
(Adapted from Rose Pacatte, *Guide to Planning In-House Film Festivals in Ten Easy Steps,* pp. 18–19)

Activity 2: Cinema Critics' Circle

In this activity, several students become movie critics, commenting from a variety of perspectives, informing audiences so that they can make good movie choices.

1. Ask some interested members of the group to be part of a Cinema Critics' Circle, either as a one-time or ongoing activity.

2. Ask the young people to choose a moderator for the group, and a name for it.

3. Select a current film in theaters, or rent one or more DVDs that teens really like.

4. Invite the students to check out reviews and ratings ahead of time, though this is not required as the goal is to develop one's own voice while respecting others' opinions.

5. Ask the teens to separately write down their criteria for judging a film, but not to share it with the others. Give them each a notebook and pen to take notes during the film.

6. Invite the rest of the group to come to the meeting of the Cinema Critics' Circle, which can be conducted as a 30 to 60 minute roundtable conversation. (With parents' permission, audio or videotape the conversation and show it for other classes or groups.)

Activity 3: Frame It!

In this activity, each student experiments with framing scenes and people with a simple paper camera, seeing for themselves the techniques and choices involved in framing a picture.

Make copies of handout 5–A, "Frame It!" and hand it out to students along with pairs of scissors. Read the objectives of the activity aloud, then ask the students to cut out the square in the camera. As they practice framing pictures with the paper camera, discuss the questions on the handout with them.

Activity 4: Media Mindfulness and the Movies

The purpose of this activity is to apply the media mindfulness strategy to the movies.

1. Pass out a copy of handout 5–B, "Movies and Media Mindfulness and the Movies," to each student.

2. Invite the young people to use the four questions to analyze a movie of their choice. (The entire group can see the same film, or this can be given as a home project.)

3. After they have written their answers to the four questions, invite them to share their responses.

Reflective Exercise

Create a contemplative environment, with soft lighting (candles burning if appropriate), and soft instrumental religious music playing. Invite the young people to still themselves. View a film clip that reminds young people of human or Gospel values. These are a few examples.

The Mission (1986, 126 minutes, rated PG). Share the scene in which Rodrigo climbs up the falls with all his weapons and armor in a sack on his back as penalty for his crimes against the native people and for killing his brother. In a powerful moment, a young Indian cuts the sack off his back, which symbolizes forgiveness by God and the native people.

Wit (2001, 98 minutes, PG-13). Share the scene in which Vivian's old professor Eve visits her in the hospital as she is dying and reads the story *The Runaway Bunny.*

Ray (2004, 178 minutes extended version, rated PG-13). Show the scene in which Ray, who has just lost his sight, cries for his mother, then investigates the kitchen and learns to "see" by hearing, touching, and using his sense of smell.

Read an appropriate Scripture passage, leave some quiet time, and then invite the young people to express how they may have experienced God's presence in the themes or characters of the film. Invite them to reflect on their own relationships with God and others in this context, and encourage them to ask forgiveness for the times they may have failed, and for strength in the future.

Closing Prayer

We praise and thank you, Lord, for the great gift of movies that tell us stories about the deepest yearnings of the human heart, and entertain and inform us. Help us to see as you see, to hear as you hear, to make mindful movie choices, and to discern your presence in the films we choose to see. Amen.

Self-Evaluation

Please fill out a copy of appendix 6–A, "Self-Evaluation," in this manual.

Cross-Curricular Connections

History. Screen two different films about the same period or event in world or United States history. Compare and contrast them according to the filmmakers' worldviews and a possible textbook depiction.

Social Justice. View a film or selected scenes that address social justice issues and connect them with the principles of Catholic social teaching (see appendix 2). Consider *Romero* (1989, 102 minutes, rated PG-13), *Entertaining Angels: The Dorothy Day Story* (1996, 112 minutes, rated PG-13), *Norma Rae* (1979, 110 minutes, rated PG), *The Long Walk Home* (1990, 97 minutes, rated PG), and *The Magnificent Seven* (1960, 128 minutes, rated PG-13).

English Literature. See the movie version, if available, of a novel that is required reading for the students—for example *Silas Marner* (George Eliot), *A Tale of Two Cities* (Charles Dickens), or *Cry, the Beloved Country* (Alan Paton). Discuss the difference between reading a book and "seeing a book."

Health. Talk about the product placement of junk food in any major motion picture, as well as alcohol and drug use.

Frame It!

Photographers take still pictures with a camera, cinematographers film the scenes that make a movie, and videographers film television shows, news, and commercials.

This is an activity that helps us understand:

- how photographers, cinematographers, and videographers choose, compose, and frame what they depict
- who or what they might leave in or leave out of the frame
- how the framing of a picture or scene might influence how we feel

Directions:

1. Cut along the dotted lines to make your own camera lens.
2. Think about the following questions and discuss them with others in your group:
- What changes do you see when you hold the paper camera at arm's length, and then hold it close to your eye?
- Walk around looking through your lens. What do you notice when you look at the same object from different angles?
- Look through a magazine or newspaper using your lens. What difference does it make when you only see part of the page or picture?

(This activity is from "Frame It!" by Rose Pacatte, in *My Friend*, October 2005, page 25, illustrated by Virginia Helen Richards and D. Thomas Halpin. Copyright © 2005 by Daughters of Saint Paul. Used with permission.)

Media Mindfulness and the Movies

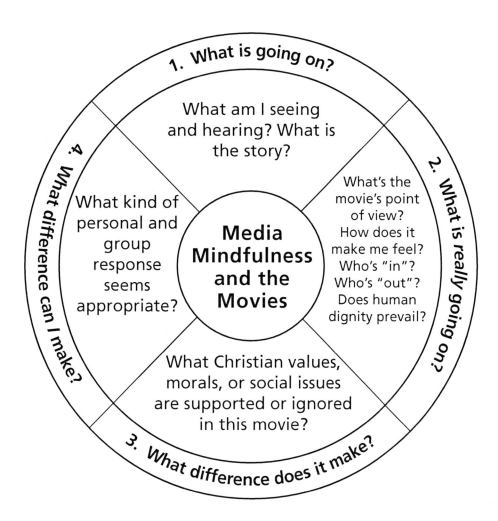

(This diagram is adapted from *Believing in a Media Culture*, by Gretchen Hailer, Thomas Zanzig, and Marilyn Kielbasa [Winona, MN: Saint Mary's Press, 1996], page 38. Copyright © 1996 by Saint Mary's Press. All rights reserved.)

Chapter 6

Music, the Music Industry, and Media Mindfulness

Introduction

Scripture Connection

> Praise him for his mighty deeds;
>> praise him according to his surpassing
>>> greatness!
>
> Praise him with trumpet sound;
>> praise him with lute and harp!
> Praise him with tambourine and dance;
>> praise him with strings and pipe!
> Praise him with clanging cymbals;
>> praise him with loud clashing cymbals!
> Let everything that breathes praise the LORD!
> Praise the LORD!

Psalm 150:2–6

This last psalm from the Book of Psalms is a joyful song thought by scripture scholars to have been performed by a complete orchestra. Too bad we have no actual music from the ancient psalms, just a few notations in some of the songs directed to the choir and musicians. The general meaning of this psalm is that everyone who breathes must praise God—every nation, race, civilization, and culture. That is what is so wonderful about the gift of music. So many genres and styles have evolved to suit every age and culture! Music really does have a way of uniting all of creation.

Session Objectives

This session will enable you to accomplish the following tasks and goals:
- to assist young people in exploring the wide range of musical genres
- to explain to them how popular music offers insight into cultural values
- to orient them to a brief history of audio technology
- to consider the Church's attitude toward music and radio
- to challenge them to apply media mindfulness to contemporary music

The music, radio, and recording industries generally value the following:
- performers with celebrity status
- instant audience appeal and emotional engagement
- recordings that sell in "hit" quantities
- in pop music, danceable rhythms or attention-grabbing lyrics that may be controversial
- clarity of sound
- planned obsolescence of technology

Things to Know About Music

In Multiple Intelligences theory, musical intelligence is the first to emerge in a child. It peaks at six, and then again at about sixteen. That is why we all can remember early nursery rhyme songs and also the songs we sang and danced to in high school—especially the songs associated with our first loves!

A Brief History of Music and Radio

Music has existed since the beginning of time. Some anthropologists believe that its primal origins began when early man and woman imitated birdsong. Music is important for children from their earliest years. Scientists have noted that babies actually turn in the womb to the sound of their mother's lullaby. One recent theory holds that if a woman plays music by Mozart during her pregnancy, the newborn will be more intelligent than other babies who lack the experience!

These are several genres and subcategories of Western music:
- classical music (sometimes called art music), including opera
- folk music, which is associated with traditional regional performers
- popular music, including rock, blues, jazz, country and western, and many more
- military or marching music
- anthems and alma maters
- hymns and other forms of religious music
- work chants
- children's songs (including traditional nursery rhymes)

Twentieth-century technology transformed music into a form of mass communication. Before audio technology, listeners could hear music only if they were in close proximity to the actual performers: singers, instrumentalists, orchestras, and so on.

Popular Music

Many say that the roots of U.S. contemporary popular music are in jazz, a uniquely American genre that began in the New Orleans area around 1900. Jazz had itself emerged from the melodies and beats of African music. Jazz style typically has an irregular rhythm, quite different from the classical music of past centuries. But jazz also spawned Dixieland, ragtime, blues, swing, rock and roll, and rap. Jazz tunes with a Latin or Caribbean style are found in dance music such as rhumba, cha-cha, reggae, merengue, and salsa. Danceability, of course, has to do not only with the melody of the music but with its beat as well. For this reason, we often find ourselves dancing to a popular song without paying much attention to the lyrics.

When we listen well, all kinds of poetic descriptions of human experiences emerge from music lyrics. As we all know, human moods have many faces: happy, sad, lonely, rejected, angry, and philosophical, for example. There are songs about love, rejection, maturing, family, work, religion, and social issues. Because most songs are about some kind of human relationship, the themes are familiar to people regardless of age, culture, or language. These kinds of songs often retain their popularity longer than others with more dated, or time-specific, lyric material.

On the darker side, there are many songs that do not present the positive side of human experience. Rather, they glorify many of the "isms" that people of faith reject. Some of their messages are racist, sexist, consumerist, vulgar, or clearly hate-filled. This side of popular music is a cause of concern for many parents and educators who see these topics as influencing youth who are still in the process of forming their own worldview. It is a part of popular music that requires a special kind of mindfulness if we are to exert the power of our faith in the face of negative lyrics.

The Music and Recording Industry

The music business, or the recording industry as it is sometimes called, is a huge international enterprise that brings in billions of dollars in revenue each year. As audio technology has evolved over the past decades, moving sound quality from downright "tinny" to marvelously clear, sales have skyrocketed throughout the world.

Many say that today, recorded music sounds better than an actual live performance. Most of us are so used to it that we fail to appreciate the history of the lowly predecessors to the MP3 and Napster generation.

The History of Music Recording

The first record player was invented around 1870 by Thomas Edison. It played music from wax cylinders about the size of a toilet-paper roll. The first disc format was the ten-inch 78 RPM record, spinning at 78 revolutions per minute, invented around 1900. Made of a shellac compound, it was as fragile as a china plate. To produce the sound, the record player's arm held a metal- or diamond-pointed needle that rode over the grooves circling the record's surface on each side. The grooves on these records were fairly wide, so a standard 78 could hold only three or four minutes of music per side.

The twelve-inch, $33^1/_3$ RPM long-playing record (also called an LP or album) was invented in the early 1920s. One LP could hold almost an hour of music. Made of vinyl plastic, these records were more flexible and less breakable than the 78s. In 1949, RCA Victor invented the 7-inch 45-RPM vinyl record, which played a single song on each side.

All of these recording formats predated the magnetic tape that many believed at the time produced far higher quality sound than from records. Initially, there were 7-inch reels with $1/_4$-inch tape and a similar sized take-up reel. Later, for convenience of storage, the card-deck-sized cassette tape was introduced. It served through the 1960s and 1970s, when the compact disc (CD) came on the market. By 1988, the CD outsold both vinyl records and cassettes! The CD has revolutionized music listening the way the DVD has changed our way of watching films.

The MPEG-1 Audio Player 3 (MP3 player) is a palm-sized encoding and compression device, invented by European engineers, that produces good sound using a minimum of data. As of 2006, Apple's iPod is one of the world's most popular brands of MP3 player. Some of these devices can upload music, photos, and videos and even offer calendar functions and other such features.

Radio as Business

From its beginning, radio became a popular vehicle for music delivery as well as for the first soap operas, and, of course, news. There is disagreement as to who actually invented radio, but the patent went to Guglielmo Marconi in 1897. The first regularly scheduled night program was broadcast in 1920. By 1940, drama and news had replaced music and local talk shows as the primary content of radio programming in the United States. With the multiplication of delivery systems as well as the commercialization of radio, the public's knowledge of, and appreciation for, music grew at an astounding rate.

In its golden era of the 1930s and 1940s, radio served the public the same way television does now. People gathered around their bulky wooden sets and listened to sports, news, music, and dramas on the networks: ABC, NBC, and CBS. Gradually, as the radio sets became smaller, they began to appear in kitchens, bedrooms, garages, and finally in automobiles.

Now the radio business tends to be more niche-oriented, as magazines are, with formats targeting particular audiences such as stay-at-home moms, teens, night workers, commuters, and the like. Some stations broadcast genres like country and western, classical, golden oldies, salsa, rhythm and blues, heavy metal, "easy listening," and foreign language programs.

Music format stations rely heavily on disk jockeys to draw large audiences to listen to the genre they promote. The top-forty stations across the country vie with one another to hire disk jockeys with edgy personalities whose banter in between songs appeals to the target audience. And once again, as in all media business, the object is sales, whether that be from advertising or music.

Radio also has its positive and negative dimensions. Talk radio can range from informative and inspirational call-in shows to uncivil, aggressive, and obscene programming hosted in the "shock jock" mode.

Radio also serves the common good, especially during all kinds of disasters. When all other communications fail, as they did during Hurricane Katrina in 2005, and during the World Trade Center attacks in 2001, amateur or ham short-wave radio operators fill in for emergency communications. The Federal Emergency Management Agency (FEMA) is now working on a unified communications frequency so that these breakdowns do not reoccur and hinder rescue efforts. Over a thousand ham radio operators helped coordinate disaster relief after Katrina.

KNOM of Nome, Alaska is a Catholic public service station of the Fairbanks diocese that reaches remote areas of western Alaska (and even into Russia). Staffed by volunteers and paid staff, the station broadcasts music, news, and inspiration and Gospel messages to people who live in darkness and isolation for several months of the year.

Getting On the Radio

How does a song get to be played on radio? The answer is, "With difficulty!" If an artist or group wants to make a top-selling recording, it not only takes a lot of persistence but also a lot of money. The process is long and tedious. First the group has to create the song, then rent a recording studio and hire a producer and sound engineer. After the actual recording, the producer creates the sound we eventually hear by "sweetening" some sounds, augmenting or erasing others. The producer makes a demonstration or demo copy of the song which is then sent to various recording companies with a request for an audition. By this time, the group should have an agent who pushes the song in the industry and tries to secure a recording contract for the group. If, in fact, the group gets a contract, it will ensure that they receive a royalty each time the song is played. Ideally the agent has also managed to secure radio play time for the group as well. This is essential for sales. If the group is lucky enough, it might win a Gold Award for selling 500,000 singles!

The Church and Music

The Church has an interesting history of accepting various musical styles. This, of course, has to do with the music that enhances the Eucharist and other sacramental celebrations. In the early days of the Church, chant was the primary musical expression used at Mass. Over the centuries, other musical genres appeared, and the Church accepted those which they deemed reverent and respectful.

In 1903, Pope St. Pius X wrote the papal *Instruction on Sacred Music (Tra le Sollecitudini)*, which offers guidelines still in effect today. He said:

> Modern music is also admitted to the Church, since it, too, furnishes compositions of such excellence, sobriety and gravity, that they are in no way unworthy of the liturgical functions.
>
> Still, since modern music has risen mainly to serve profane uses, greater care must be taken with regard to it, in order that the musical compositions of modern style which are admitted in the Church may contain nothing profane, be free from reminiscences of motifs adopted in the theaters, and be not fashioned even in their external forms after the manner of profane pieces. (No. 5)

Characteristics of the Music, Radio, and Recording Industries

- seek mass appeal through star performers
- market a variety of genres to various audiences; big business
- value technical excellence in sound quality
- promote changing technologies such as satellite and podcasting
- present controversial content and personalities that can help sell the product
- engage in public service

Things to Remember When Talking with Teens About Music

- Do encourage young people to use music to decrease stress.
- Do not put down their music choices.
- Do listen to music they suggest.
- Do not rank musical genres, because all have audiences.
- Do encourage them to find out about the personal values of pop stars.
- Do incorporate popular music into educational settings.
- Do inquire what radio stations they and their parents listen to and why.

Movies About Music and Radio

Use clips from these films to illustrate a point or begin a conversation, or show an entire film to your group and analyze it together.

Walk the Line (2005, 136 minutes, rated PG-13). This film follows the life story of American singer-songwriter Johnny Cash until his marriage to June Carter.

Selena (1997, 127 minutes, rated PG-13). This movie follows the life of the young and very popular Tejano singer Selena Quintanilla-Perez, who became a star through the support of her family, but was killed in 1995 at the age of twenty-three, by the president of her fan club.

Radio (2003, 109 minutes, rated PG). Based on a true story, this film tells of a small town football coach's friendship with a mentally challenged boy who never goes anywhere without his radio.

Frequency (2000, 118 minutes, rated PG-13 for disturbing and violent images). In this science-fiction story, a New York City firefighter finds he can communicates across time via a short-wave radio and talks with his father, a man he barely knew.

Media Saints and Greats

Saint Cecilia (second century) was a Roman martyr often associated with singing and playing musical instruments. She is said to have been singing while she was martyred.

Pope Saint Gregory the Great (540–604) collected ancient melodies and chants that were later referred to as Gregorian chant.

Media Detective

Give these interesting and fun assignments to your students so they can investigate the media. Have them report back!

- Find out who won the Grammy Award last year for Best Album.
- Find out who won the Grammy for Best Male Country Vocal Performance.
- Find out why the Grammy Award has that name.
- Find the number-one-selling song in American history.
- Find out the name of the dog on the RCA Victor logo.
- Find out the first winner of the Diamond Award for sales.
- Find out about the difference between FM, AM, satellite radio, and "streaming online" broadcasting.
- Find out about Vatican Radio: its history and its programming.
- Find out about the Catholic radio stations in your area.
- Find out what NPR stands for, and listen to it for a while.
- Find out what the Gabriel Awards are.
- Find out which awards are given to top radio stations and personalities.

Activities

Activity 1: Experiencing a Variety of Sound Recordings

In this activity, the young people listen to vinyl records and a CD to assess the quality of sound and the importance of this quality.

1. In preparation for this activity, find a three-speed phonograph (78, 33 ⅓, and 45 RPM) and the corresponding size records. (Visit a radio museum if one is in your area.)

2. Play each record for the group. Ask the young people to discuss the quality of sound of the records and have them identify which record seems best.

3. Then play a music CD on a good audio system. Discuss sound quality. How much does it matter, and why?

Activity 2: A Mixed-Generation Dance

In this activity, students host a mixed-generation dance so that attendees can listen to songs across the decades, sing them, and dance to them with mentoring from couples who were teens in those particular decades.

Divide your group into committees to plan a mixed-generation dance at your school or parish. You should have these committees:

- publicity
- DJ selection
- popular music from today
- danceable songs from each decade since the 1930s
- refreshments

Engage the group's imagination by suggesting that grandparents, parents, uncles, aunts, cousins, teachers, and friends be invited!

Activity 3: Song Critique

In this activity, the young people critique songs they bring in for this purpose. Set parameters for their music choice as appropriate.

1. Have students bring in CDs of their favorite pop music, then give a copy of handout 6–A, "Be a Song Critic!," to each person.

2. Group the students into pairs or groups of three. Ask each team to talk among themselves about the music they brought and to choose one song to share with the entire group.

3. Gather the young people back together. Explain the headings on the handout chart. Play each song for the entire group and after each one, ask the students to evaluate it using this form.

4. Invite several students to present their evaluations for a larger group discussion of various interpretations of the songs. Invite students to share about any insights they gained during this activity.

Activity 4: Media Mindfulness and Music Assessment

In this activity, young people apply the strategy of media mindfulness to popular music.
Invite students to select music that they like to listen to, perhaps asking the group to select a genre such as dance music, love songs, or scores from movies. Have them use handout 6–B, "Media Mindfulness and Music" to reflect on the music.

Reflective Exercise

Create a quiet space. Arrange, if possible, to have a large cross on the ground in the center of the group. Surround the cross with votive candles. Ask the students to sit or kneel around the cross on the floor. Play a recording of the chants of the ecumenical monastery of Taize. Invite the group to join in the chants. Let the activity last about ten minutes. Recite a short prayer to end the exercise.

Closing Prayer

Creator God, you have given us the marvelous gift of music and song. Help us appreciate the talents of those who share their music with us. May we discover in their songs the values which we profess as Christians and reject any values that lead us from the Gospel path. Amen.

Cross-Curricular Connections

 Music. Play several classical pieces for the students. Ask them which one they prefer and why.

 History. Have the students research how traditional African American spirituals were also communication tools.

Religion. Teach the students a short Gregorian chant and show them what it looks like in print.

Self-Evaluation

Please fill out a copy of handout appendix 6, "Self-Evaluation," in this manual.

Be a Song Critic!

Team #			
Artist			
Title			
Genre			
Melody Grade	Excellent Good Poor	Excellent Good Poor	Excellent Good Poor
Lyrics Value	Best 5 4 3 2 1 Worst	Best 5 4 3 2 1 Worst	Best 5 4 3 2 1 Worst
Emotional Effect	Best 5 4 3 2 1 Worst	Best 5 4 3 2 1 Worst	Best 5 4 3 2 1 Worst
Comments			

Media Mindfulness and Music

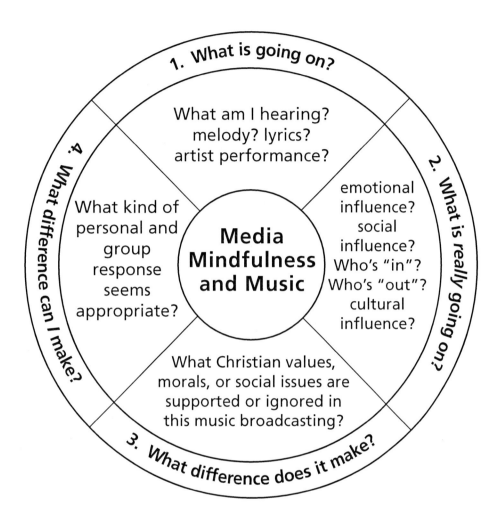

1. What is going on?

What am I hearing? melody? lyrics? artist performance?

2. What is really going on?

emotional influence? social influence? Who's "in"? Who's "out"? cultural influence?

Media Mindfulness and Music

4. What difference can I make?

What kind of personal and group response seems appropriate?

3. What difference does it make?

What Christian values, morals, or social issues are supported or ignored in this music broadcasting?

(This diagram is adapted from *Believing in a Media Culture*, by Gretchen Hailer, Thomas Zanzig, and Marilyn Kielbasa [Winona, MN: Saint Mary's Press, 1996], page 38. Copyright © 1996 by Saint Mary's Press. All rights reserved.)

Chapter 7

Television and Media Mindfulness

Introduction

Scripture Connection

> While I was speaking in prayer, the man Gabriel, whom I had seen before in a vision, came to me in swift flight at the time of the evening sacrifice. He came and said to me, "Daniel, I have now come out to give you wisdom and understanding." (Daniel 9:21–22)

The Book of Daniel was written around the year 167 BC. Its hero is Daniel along with his three companions who were faithful to God's word in the face of adversity and temptation. Here, Daniel is praying and the angel Gabriel comes to teach him. Saint Gabriel is one of the patron saints of television—a word that literally means "to see at a distance." Indeed, television entertains us by telling us stories from a distance; it may also inform us about adversity and temptation. Daniel and his friends are examples of heroes who choose what is good.

Session Objectives

This session will enable you to accomplish the following tasks and goals:
- to become aware of the history of television and its role in our lives
- to appreciate television as a gift of God
- to understand television as a business
- to reflect on television ratings and censorship
- to be aware of the role of government in the television industry
- to consider effective responses to television
- to know better the Church's attitude towards television

What Is Television?

Television is an increasingly digitalized telecommunications system that uses air waves, cable, and satellite to transmit sound and images—mostly in the forms of information and entertainment programming—between a transmitter and a receiver.

The television industry generally values the following:

- profitability, notably through advertising sales
- compelling stories told through entertainment programming
- early reporting of breaking news in news broadcasting
- broadcasting sports in a way that maximizes audiences

Things to Know About Television

A Brief History of Television

Television was not invented by a single person. The foundations were laid in 1831, when American scientist Joseph Henry and British scientist Michael Faraday independently discovered electromagnetic induction. Decades later, when the technology became available, several scientists around the world focused on inventing a medium that would carry images, sound, and movement from a central facility to a multitude of receivers.

The word *television* was used for the first time in 1900 at the International Congress on Electricity during the World's Fair in Paris. The United States government and Bell Telephone made the first long-distance broadcast between New York and Washington, D.C., in 1927. At age fifteen, Philo Farnsworth invented the first complete television system, which he named the Image Dissector, and filed for a patent that same year.

In 1930, the British Broadcasting Corporation (BBC) began regular television transmissions, and in 1933 the University of Iowa started broadcasting twice a week. By 1936, about two hundred television sets were in use around the world.

In 1960, 87.3 percent of American households had at least one TV (U.S. Census, 1960). The United States Census Bureau determined that in 2001 there were 248 million television sets in the United States. 98.2 percent of U.S. households had one television and the average home had 2.4 sets.

Television, Democracy, and Social Justice in the United States

The Federal Communications Commission (FCC) was established as an independent government agency by the Communications Act of 1934 to protect the public interest and to prevent monopolies. Responsible only to Congress, its mission still is to regulate national communications, to serve the public interest in relation to television, radio, satellite, and cable in the United States and its territories. Although the FCC's tasks have grown to include the Internet and cellular communications, its major mission today is to monitor live broadcast media and respond to the public's concerns about offensive content. To avoid business monopolies—as well as ideological ones—the FCC regulates the consolidation of the television and radio stations; it also levies fines for such infractions as Janet Jackson's now famous "wardrobe malfunction" during the Superbowl half-time program on February 1, 2004.

Deregulation

The deregulation of television that occurred under President Ronald Reagan's administration changed the ways the FCC governs the television industry. In 1987, Reagan vetoed the efforts of Congress to put the FCC's policy, "the fairness doctrine," into law. This policy required broadcasters to address controversial issues and provide opportunities for those with other opinions to respond. Reagan's veto changed the role of television stations, which up to this time had been considered "trustees" of the public airwaves.

In the early 1980s, legislation regulating ownership of television stations was changed, increasing the number of stations that could be owned by one entity. With single ownership of many news and entertainment outlets, only one point of view becomes the dominant voice people experience.

There are several monopolies within the broadcasting industry. Australian-born American multibillionaire Rupert Murdoch created News Corp and now controls a vast multinational media empire that includes holdings in Australia, England, and Asia, American book and newspaper publishing companies, the Fox News Channel included in the Fox Network, and about twenty channels across the country.

Another media giant is General Electric, the parent company to NBC and the owner of other media companies such as Universal Pictures and Universal Parks and Resorts. As of January 2006, the Walt Disney Company was the second largest media conglomerate in the world, second only to Time Warner. Although these corporations continually "morph" by breaking up and selling off companies, or acquiring new ones to create gigantic new entities under different names, the fact is that media monopolization is a powerful trend.

When an economic and ideological mega-media monopoly is allowed to exist, or to coexist with as few as four or five others, only a minimal number of perspectives are broadcast to the audience or citizens at any given time, on any given issue. Because broadcast, print, cable, and satellite communications are primarily one-way, and backed by large economic forces, this kind of electronic communication has the power to dominate public discourse and opinion.

The FCC also attempts to regulate what is appropriate in programming and advertising. It bans obscene material and restricts broadcasts of indecent material during the hours in which young children will be watching television. This can be a somewhat arbitrary exercise and dependent on the reaction of Congress and the public, as it was in the case of Janet Jackson at the Super Bowl.

Monopolies threaten social justice for all. Because of media deregulation, the public airwaves in the United States no longer protect public service and welfare nor provide equal access that has the potential to give all citizens a voice. Even though community access cable stations are available, few people really make use of them, and even fewer ac-

tually watch them. When social justice is at stake, believers have a responsibility to discern, discuss, and take appropriate action so that all people, regardless of race, culture, creed, gender, age, religion, or social class, can have a voice in the perspectives presented in all news and entertainment.

Television and Business

In the United States, radio and television have always depended on advertising dollars to pay for programming. Some cable and satellite channels do not carry advertising but instead, subscribers pay a fee for access to their programs and movies. PBS (the Public Broadcasting System) is noncommercial and largely paid for by donations from the Corporation for Public Broadcasting, and grants from private foundations and the federal government. We still hear that "This program is underwritten by . . ." but, of course, sponsorship is also a type of advertising.

Television Commercials

Advertisers seek to link their products with good feelings so that once they have the demographics, they can carefully place their commercials to create the needed relationship between the viewers' wants, needs, and emotions. For example, if a primetime television drama is controversial for a large part of its audience, an advertiser might pull its spots from the program—not because of its own judgment of the content, but to avoid any association with negative or uncomfortable feelings. People are more apt to buy products they feel good about, even if they don't need them.

Television advertising, first and foremost, teaches us to buy. It is big business because it delivers messages about its products directly into people's homes. It often creates a need—softer toilet paper, designer cat food, home-delivered fast food—and then offers a way to meet that need.

Television commercials use five primary techniques to get our attention and make us feel good about their products: humor, babies and little children, animals, sex appeal, and a focus on what's "cool." Advertisers place their products in and around programs that appeal to their sought-after demographic. For example, cars and trucks are advertised during prime time when there is a large male audience with disposable income (between the ages of 18 and 50).

Embedding products in television shows and movies to enhance brand recognition has become a normal practice. For example, the movie *The Truman Show* (1998, 103 minutes, rated PG) made fun of the practice in both media. (The film itself is an excellent meditation on the role of television in modern life.) A new genre of television shows began in 2003 with *Extreme Makeover: Home Edition*. While rebuilding the home of a deserving family, the program showcases products from sponsoring corporations. This is embedded advertising at its height, because shows like this spark our sympathy and make us associate certain products with helping a family begin again. On the other hand, shows such as this one may be what responsible capitalism looks like in a consumer society.

Television Ratings and Censorship

Responding to complaints from parents about inappropriate programming accessible to children, the television industry has adopted a rating system for programming. This system is meant to help parents and guardians censor and monitor their child's viewing, especially in association with the V-chip.

Since 2000, all television sets 13 inches or larger that are manufactured in the United States have a V-Chip installed. When the V-chip is programmed according to the ratings, programs can be blocked and the system controlled by a parental password. The ratings systems for television (and other media) are created by the industry to avoid governmental control, but are often hotly contested by parents and academics. The ratings and V-chip place the responsibility for what children see

squarely on the shoulders of parents and guardians. The industry has yet to address its own responsibility for the programming it creates.

Ratings and reviews provide guidance, and a technological device such as the V-chip can *control* what kids watch. But these are no substitute for parental participation in their children's viewing, which includes talking with children about *why* programs are appropriate or not. Control is for the moment; communication is for life.

Responding to Unsuitable Media

When a program is aired that is generally inappropriate or contrary to your values, the most important thing to do is to talk about it with your family, students, or youth group and articulate *why* you judge it to be unsuitable.

Some concerned people write letters or send e-mails to the local stations, the national network offices, or the Federal Trade Commission, whose job it is to protect consumers. Another approach people take is to communicate with a program's sponsors if they are unhappy about a program or commercial—once they have actually seen it. We lose credibility if we react before seeing a program, rather than responding afterwards.

Media boycotts can absorb much time and energy but have limited value, because they often pique public curiosity, and corporate executives may not even know they are happening. Boycots often serve merely to make the boycotters feel that they are making a difference, rather than actually challenging those in the entertainment business to be original, creative, and artistic.

Rather than simply complaining about, or reacting to, poor programming, responsible citizens and Christians are called to respond in a positive way to programming that reflects Gospel values. These shows will not be developed or renewed otherwise. For example, *Joan of Arcadia* ran for two seasons, 2003 through 2005, but the show was not renewed. Pastors, teachers, youth ministers, and parents could have made this show a success and kept a religious and spiritual program in prime time, but because they did not know the show was in jeopardy or did not know their voice needed to be heard, the show was discontinued. As Christians, we are called to celebrate and reinforce the good.

Archbishop John P. Foley said this to the Pontifical Council for Social Communications in March 2006:

As many of us know all too well the communications community has often expected and too often received from the Church more condemnation than commendation, more negative criticism than positive affirmation. The fact that the Church has often been correct in its criticisms has not diminished their sting. The fact that many good productions have gone unrecognized has intensified the hurt from the criticisms. Let us continue not so much to curse the darkness as to offer the light of Christ through the communications media to those searching for purpose in life and love—because "Deus Caritas Est," God is love.

An Effective and Responsible Catholic Response to Television

See handout appendix 3–B, "What Is an Effective and Responsible Catholic Response to Television?" in order to share such an approach with young people and their parents.

The Church and Television

In 1957, Pope Pius XII issued the Church's first official document about television, an encyclical letter titled *On Motion Pictures, Radio, and Television* (*Miranda Prorsus*). The Vatican II *Decree on the Media of Social Communications* (*Inter Mirifica*, December 4, 1963) spoke about all the media available at that time, and the possibility of those to come. While these documents acknowledge media as gifts, they mention the inherent spiritual, political, and social

dangers of their use as well. *Inter Mirifica* expressed optimism that television (and other media) could be a means of evangelization and promoting to the Church, the faithful, and humanity.

There is no doubt, however, that the Vatican II document strongly encourages the Church at all levels to use the media to proclaim the Gospel. Later documents, especially *Dawn of a New Era (Aetatis Novae)* in 1992 encouraged the faithful to be prophetic about their use of the media, notably television. It asked them to become critically engaged in the production and consumption of programming through media literacy education from a Christian perspective that is media mindfulness.

The Church believes that television is always teaching us something through information, advertising, and entertainment. Television, indeed all media, can be used for good and human advancement, or for political and economic dominance through productions that promote materialistic values and images or stories that degrade human dignity. Often these elements can exist side by side in the same program or series. Media mindfulness gives us the skills to tell the difference.

Characteristics of Television

- is easily accessible in the United States
- evokes emotion through news, dramas, and other types of programming
- teaches us to buy and can create a sense of entitlement
- can imply that behaviors that are contrary to human dignity, the Gospels, and Church teaching are normal and acceptable
- Teaches audiences as it entertains; entertains as it teaches
- reflects all types of values
- is one-way communication, because the audience does not have the means to respond in the same way that television reaches the audience
- reinforces or challenges racial, gender, age, vocational, religious, and social stereotypes
- tells the audience what is important

- can generate charitable support for victims of natural disasters
- can be good company for the lonely, the isolated, the aged, and the infirm

Movies About Television

Use clips from these films to illustrate a point or begin a conversation, or your group could see an entire movie and analyze it together.

The Truman Show (1998, 103 minutes, rated PG). In this film, an insurance salesman discovers his whole life has been broadcast on television.

Pleasantville (1998, 124 minutes, rated PG-13). Two teens are sucked into the set of a 1950s family sitcom in black and white.

Mr. Mom (1983, 91 minutes, rated PG). In this comedy, a dad stays home and gets hooked on soap operas while his wife goes to work.

Good Night and Good Luck (2005, 93 minutes, rated PG). This is the true story of Edward R. Murrow, the father of investigative reporting on television, who challenged the culture of fear propagated by Senator Joseph McCarthy's hunt for communists in the 1950s.

The Insider (1999, 157 minutes, R for language). This feature film tells how an episode of CBS's *60 Minutes* about the wrongdoings of the U.S. tobacco industry was not aired because Westinghouse was negotiating the purchase of CBS at the time and the network's lawyers thought this episode would interfere. (Though this movie is rated R, the authors of this book do recommend showing it in its entirety. Review the movie and if you decide to show it, request permission from the young people's parents or guardians, explaining the reason for showing the film, the rating, and the value of the film.)

Things to Remember When Talking with Teens About Television

- Do keep in mind that young people sixteen and older watch television less than those who are younger.
- Do not give them the impression you are being unfair about or dislike television or they will automatically defend it instead of questioning it.
- Do not assume you know what the young people like or what their television habits are.
- Do survey them to find out their media likes, dislikes, and habits.
- Do not disapprove of their media preferences or they will "edit" their responses to what they think you want to hear.
- Do watch some programs popular with teens and then ask their opinion about which shows they think are good and why, and which they think are bad for themselves or their younger siblings and why.

Media Saints and Greats

Saint Clare of Assisi (1194–1253) founded the Franciscan Order of Poor Clares. One Christmas Eve she was ill and had to stay in bed at the monastery during midnight Mass. She was very sad to miss it, and while praying, she had a vision of the Mass's being celebrated. Because she "saw from a distance," she was later named one of the patrons of television and television writers as well.

Saint Gabriel the Archangel was God's messenger many times in the Scriptures, especially when he announced to Mary that she would be the mother of God. As such, Gabriel has been named a patron of telecommunications, especially television.

Media Detective

Give these interesting and fun assignments to your students so they can investigate the media. Have them report back!

- Find out who Vladimir Zworykin was and what he did.
- Find out who the head of the FCC is.
- Find out how many companies Rupert Murdoch, General Electric, and the Walt Disney Corporation own, and list them.
- Find out the prices of a 30-second and a 60-second commercial for this year's Super Bowl and March Madness, and compare them to last year's.
- Find out what public service announcements the main broadcast networks are airing at this time.
- Find out in what year cigarette commercials were banned from television in the United States and why.
- Find out about how the Nielsen TV ratings really work.
- Find out about awards for television excellence.

Activities

Activity 1: Analyzing Television Commercials

This activity helps students develop critical skills for thinking about TV commercials, and talk about their opinions while respecting others'.

1. Record and watch an hour-long television drama in preparation for this activity.

2. Watch the show with the group. Ask the students to count all the commercials from the beginning of the program to the beginning of the next program, and note what they are about.

3. In a large-group discussion, talk about these subjects.

- What audiences are the advertisers trying to reach? Consider age, race, social status, gender.
- What techniques do the commercials use to get your attention?
- What is the worldview of the television series? That is, what is its social, economic, political, or religious point of view, if any? What story is it telling, and what are the characteristics of its audience?
- How does the show make you feel? Why?
- What techniques does the show use to keep your attention? Does the show respect women and diverse cultures and races? Are people of diverse cultures present?

3. Ask one group to write a review of the program and another group to write a review of the commercials, keeping in mind the core concepts of media literacy (see the introduction of this book) as well as principles of Catholic social teaching (see appendix 2). After sharing these reviews, follow up with these questions:

- Would you recommend the show to others? Why or why not?
- Would you buy any of the items or services advertised? Why or why not?
- What ads are the most entertaining? Which products are you most likely to buy? Why?

Activity 2: Soap Opera Spoof Production

In this activity, the young people create a parody of a daily soap opera, keeping in mind the media mindfulness strategy they have learned.

Note: First review your school or diocese's policy about filming young people, and send out permission slips to parents or fulfill any other policy requirements.

This production activity is for the entire group. It can be presented as a television show and videotaped (with parental permission, if required), or presented on the stage. The aim is to produce a show that is a parody, and to create and perform commercials that are socially just, keeping in mind two criteria: comedy and human dignity. Note that this is also an opportunity to be creative, to collaborate, and to communicate as Christians. Explain storyboarding and have teams draw a sequence of of scenes that convey the storyline (as shown on handout 8–A). (Evaluate the production and process after with the group, according to the criteria noted.)

1. Assign some key roles. Appoint them, ask for volunteers, or have groups elect them: a director, a producer (manager), a casting director, and writers. Everyone else will serve on the cast or the production team.

2. Pass out handout 7–A, "Soap Opera Spoof Production Check Sheet."

3. The whole group can decide which soap(s) to parody in half an hour, and which commercials to create or parody as well.

4. Divide tasks and create a schedule, working backwards from the production date so people will have their tasks done on time.

5. Promote the event if you intend to invite an audience.

6. Consider using two or three video cameras for analysis of perspective, point of view, and so forth. Discuss the process and results with the students, using media mindfulness criteria.

Activity 3: Television Clip Showcase

This activity invites the young people to focus on a television show more closely as individuals, to critique it, and talk about it with others.

1. Ask each of the young people to tape a television program of their choice. It can be sports, a sitcom, primetime drama, or other genre. Tell them to select one brief scene or commercial (2 to 3 minutes maximum length) to show to the group the following week. Ask that they be ready to explain why they liked the clip, did not like it, or thought it was interesting, and why.

2. Each presenter should first briefly explain the context of the clip, adding any background relevant to the discussion.

3. After the clip is shown, have the presenter briefly assess it and then ask the group to analyze it according to audience, worldview, values, social justice implications, and so forth.

4. Conclude the session by summarizing the main that the young people raised, and by voting for the clip that best respects human dignity and for the one that is most entertaining.

Activity 4: Media Mindfulness and Television

The purpose of this activity is to apply the strategy of media mindfulness to television shows and commercials. See handout 7–B, "Media Mindfulness and Television."

Reflective Exercise: Praying the News

In preparation for this activity, tape the evening news the night before this experience.

Create a quiet space. Place the Scriptures on a table in front of the television monitor, or near the screen. Ask the students to read a Gospel passage that sound like news, such as Matthew 24:6–7 or John 6:1–8.

Show the main news stories from the beginning to the first commercial break. Invite the group to reflect on these stories and the Scriptures and to share their thoughts in the form of intercessory prayers. Conclude the prayer experience by praying the Our Father together.

Closing Prayer

Through drama, comedy, and news, television programs let us share the joys and pains of all human living. Saint Clare, patroness of television, you saw the Mass from a distance one Christmas when you were too ill to go to church. Intercede for us so that what we choose to see from a distance may help us be better human beings, brothers and sisters to those in need, and responsible citizens who work for justice and peace. Amen.

Self-Evaluation

Please fill out a copy of handout appendix 6–A, "Self-Evaluation," in this manual.

Cross-Curricular Connections

Geography. Watch TV nightly news programs with your students and have them record which countries are mentioned over the period of a week. Then look at the globe or a map, and make observations about which countries receive attention and which do not.

History. Compare and contrast two television documentaries about the same historical event and seek explanations for any differences. For example, *Joan of Arc* on the History Channel and *Joan of Arc: Child of War, Soldier of God* (Faith and Values/Hallmark) are good films to compare and are widely available.

Health. Have the students document and analyze all food ads that they see over a week, using the key questions of media literacy on Handout 7–B, "Media Mindfulness and Television."

Mathematics. Research the Nielsen TV ratings and talk about how they work and how advertisers and television networks use them.

Theology. Select several prime-time television dramas and watch them with the young people. Ask them to look for any type of message that is Gospel-like or any figure who resembles Jesus.

Soap Opera Spoof Production Check Sheet

Due date

_____

Director

_____

Producer

_____

Casting director

_____

Writers

_____

Title of show

_____

Production date

_____

Soap opera(s) to spoof

_____

Commercials

_____

_____

Cast list

_____

_____

_____

Production team
    Videographers

_____

    Costume manager

_____

    Set decoration team

_____

    Sound technician

_____

    Lighting

_____

Notes:

Media Mindfulness and Television

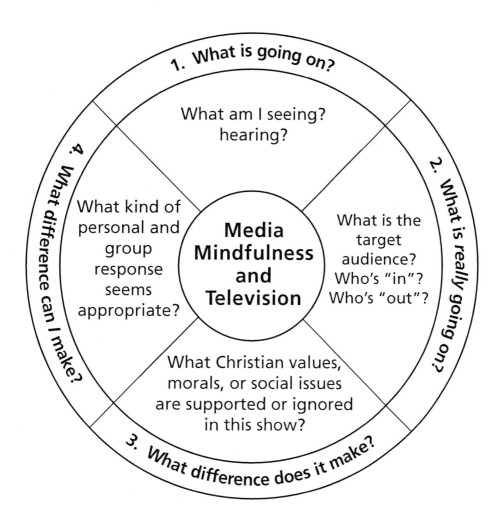

1. **What is going on?**

What am I seeing? hearing?

2. **What is really going on?**

What is the target audience? Who's "in"? Who's "out"?

3. **What difference does it make?**

What Christian values, morals, or social issues are supported or ignored in this show?

4. **What difference can I make?**

What kind of personal and group response seems appropriate?

Media Mindfulness and Television

(This diagram is adapted from *Believing in a Media Culture*, by Gretchen Hailer, Thomas Zanzig, and Marilyn Kielbasa [Winona, MN: Saint Mary's Press, 1996], page 38. Copyright © 1996 by Saint Mary's Press. All rights reserved.)

Chapter 8

Electronic Games and Media Mindfulness

Introduction

Scripture Connection

> Jacob was left alone; and a man wrestled with him until daybreak. When the man saw that he did not prevail against Jacob, he struck him on the hip socket; and Jacob's hip was put out of joint as he wrestled with him. Then he said, "Let me go, for the day is breaking." But Jacob said, "I will not let you go, unless you bless me." So he said to him, "What is your name?" And he said, "Jacob." Then the man said, "You shall no longer be called Jacob, but Israel, for you have striven with God and with humans, and have prevailed." Then Jacob asked him, "Please tell me your name." But he said, "Why is it that you ask my name?" And there he blessed him. So Jacob called the place Peniel, saying, "For I have seen God face to face, and yet my life is preserved." The sun rose upon him as he passed Penuel, limping because of his hip. (Gen. 32:24–31)

Jacob is a patriarch of the Old Testament whose story and example continue to lead us to our belief in the one true God. In this passage, an angel struggles with Jacob, and Jacob comes to realize that his opponent is the Lord. Jacob just left his father-in-law, Laban. Now, Jacob and his family, with all his servants and belongings, have just crossed over the Jordan River into the Promised Land where Jacob will have new struggles. The angel wrestled with Jacob until he had no strength left, a sign that God will be Jacob's strength in the years and trials to come.

Often based on hero-quest stones, many electronic video games present similar scenarios because the hero must pass from one level to the next, proving his or her character or strength in order to move on towards the goal.

Session Objectives

This session will enable you to accomplish the following tasks and goals:
- to acquaint young people with a brief history of electronic games
- to investigate the communication aspects of electronic games
- to critically examine electronic games
- to think about ways to use such games wisely
- to explore the games' various elements
- to consider the Church's attitude towards leisure and electronic games

> ## What Are Electronic Games?
>
> A game is an activity carried out for amusement, often competitively, and often involving a strategy carried out to achieve an end. "The term 'electronic games' refers to games played on TV consoles (such as Sony's PlayStation2, Nintendo's Game-Cube and Microsoft's Xbox), personal computers, handheld game units, mobile phones, public arcade game machines and other similar electronic game units." (Don Lee, "Video Game Types Defined")

Electronic game designers generally value these kinds of games:

- games that entertain with compelling stories and characters
- games that challenge players' intelligence and build skills
- fast games that develop eye-hand coordination
- creative games that dazzle with computer generated images (CGIs)
- games that give players an exaggerated sense of power; this may include violence, blood, and gore
- profitable games that build customer loyalty

Things to Know About Electronic Games

The History of Electronic Games

Unlike some other media, these games have a relatively short history.

The Early Years

Physicist Willy Higinbotham invented the very first video game in 1958. It was a table tennis game, and he played it on an oscilloscope—very unlike contemporary video games. In 1961, a student at the Massachusetts Institute of Technology invented Spacewar, the very first interactive computer game.

Then Nolan Bushnell and Ted Dabney took *Spacewar* and created an arcade version called *Computer Space*. People thought it was too hard to play, but fifteen hundred games were sold anyway.

Bushnell and Dabney founded Atari in 1972. The first video game they created was called *Pong* (more table tennis) and 150,000 units were produced. *Death Race* was the game that started debate about violence in games. *Gunfight* was the first computer game that used a microprocessor (chip). In 1976, the first video game console was sold that allowed players to change games by exchanging cartridges. In the latter part of this decade, people began playing games on home computers and could buy consoles to use at home.

The 1980s

In the 1980s, many companies competed for this hot new market of gaming devices and the games created for them. In 1980, *Battlezone* became the first 3-D game ever created; it was set in a virtual battlefield. The United States government later adapted it for military training exercises. In the same year, 300,000 units of the arcade game *Pac-Man* were released worldwide and *Defender*, the first virtual reality game, was launched.

In 1981, the field's first magazine was started: *Electronic Games*. The first video game to use laser-disc technology (an optic disc storage system) came out the same year Nintendo was released in Japan. Nintendo (some Internet sites translate it roughly as "Leave luck to heaven" or "In heaven's hands"), a video game delivery system, was not sold in the United States until 1985. *Tetris*, a game played on a personal computer, was developed by a Russian programmer named Alex Pajitnov. In 1989, Nintendo released the handheld Game Boy, a game console.

The 1990s

In 1993, the United States Senate launched an investigation into video-game violence, resulting in the formation of the Entertainment Software Rating Board a year later. The ratings this board established continue to appear on game packaging.

In 1994, the Sega Saturn and the Sony PlayStation consoles were released in Japan and by 1997, twenty million PlayStations had been sold worldwide. In 1997, the precursor to the PDA (personal digital assistant) was developed.

In 1999, Billy Mitchell of New Hampshire attained the highest possible score a *Pac-Man* player could reach: 3,333,360. He managed this by passing through all 256 levels of the game; it took him over six hours.

Electronic Games from 2000 to 2006

In 2000, *The Sims* became the bestselling PC game ever. In 2001, Microsoft released the Xbox console and Nintendo released GameCube and Game Boy Advance, which is portable. In December 2005, Microsoft released its Xbox 360. Some young adults waited in line for more than 70 hours to be the first to buy it. The system quickly sold out, and it became one of the hottest items ever auctioned on eBay.

Electronic Games as Means of Communication

Electronic games, played alone or with others, online or offline, are a means of entering into the world of mass communication. Ideas and values are always being communicated, even through the packaging, homepages, and story scenarios. For example, that we even possess the means to buy these games signifies that we accept the values of consumerism to a certain extent. The way the games are played can convey and reinforce individualism and isolation. Their anonymity can result in the failure to take responsibility for the roles we play in electronic games, the money we may squander, the risk to self and others, and so forth.

Electronic games can be fun; they can bring people to collaborate together or against one another in competition. In some cases, these players can be the same room or on the other side of the world. They can also be used excessively, unwisely, and uncritically. Choosing to use them thus can affect our lives in negative ways, even to the extreme.

Games such as *Grand Theft Auto* (or any of its various spinoffs) teach, through vicarious experience, extreme violence toward others, especially women, online and offline. (Although the most extreme violent content is not immediately visible, players can unlock this violent sexual content). According to the values of media mindfulness, spending time simulating sexual violence is never a good option: it violates one's own human dignity and that of others.

When immature or vulnerable people engage in such games with no restrictions or parental supervision, they can become a danger to themselves and others. For example, eighteen-year old Devin Moore from Alabama played *Grand Theft Auto* compulsively and in 2003 murdered three people following a pattern similar to the game's. Ed Bradley of *60 Minutes* interviewed Dr. David Walsh of the National Institute of Media and the Family about Moore, brain research, and video games. The segment, titled "Can a Video Game Lead to Murder?" aired on March 6, 2005.

Ed Bradley:

> David Walsh, a child psychologist who's coauthored a study connecting violent video games to physical aggression, says the link can be explained in part by pioneering brain research recently done at the National Institutes of Health—which shows that the teenage brain is not fully developed.
>
> Does repeated exposure to violent video games have more of an impact on a teenager than it does on an adult?

Dr. Walsh:

> It does. And that's largely because the teenage brain is different from the adult brain. The impulse control center of the brain, the part of

the brain that enables us to think ahead, consider consequences, manage urges—that's the part of the brain right behind our forehead called the prefrontal cortex. That's under construction during the teenage years. In fact, the wiring of that is not completed until the early 20s."

This compulsive game playing, added to other social factors—for example, unstable family life—can influence young and socially vulnerable people for whom the real-life acting-out of virtual or fantasy scenarios makes sense.

The Church and Electronic Games

The Church has not yet directly addressed electronic games or human behavior in relation to them. General principles of Christian morality apply to all human activity, including leisure. Only people who have the time and access during their days or hours off from work or school can engage in electronic games. As Christians, we have the right to enjoy leisure activities that help renew us, but we also have responsibilities regarding the poor—who have neither time for leisure nor access to activities like electronic gaming.

The morality of leisure is concerned with the nature and content of the activities in which we engage. Therefore, for followers of Christ, critical awareness and media mindfulness skills are useful life strategies when applied to the games we choose to enjoy. The pastoral instruction *On the Means of Social Communication* (*Communio et Progressio*, 1971) offers food for thought about the place of electronic games in our culture today:

> Today, through the media, the noblest forms of artistic expression offer true recreation—in the fullest sense of that word—to more and more people. And there is more and more call for this in our complex society. Simple entertainment, too, has a value of its own. It lightens the burden of daily problems and it occupies men's leisure. The wide variety of productions that the

> media offer for these hours of leisure is in fact a remarkable service to mankind. But recipients should exercise self-control. They must not allow themselves to be so beguiled by the charms of the media's products or by the curiosity that these arouse that they neglect urgent duties or simply waste time. (No. 52)

Characteristics of Electronic Games

- are profitable as a business
- can teach problem solving-skills
- can build hand-eye coordination
- can evoke intense emotions
- are fun and relaxing in moderation
- can be addictive
- can blur the boundaries between the real world and the virtual world
- can isolate the player from family and responsibilities

Movies About Electronic Games

Use clips from these films to illustrate a point or begin a conversation, or show an entire film to your group and analyze it together.

The Net (1995, 114 minutes, rated PG-13). This is the story of Angela, a computer whiz who gets embroiled in a computer conspiracy.

S1mOne (2002, 117 minutes, rated PG-13). A washed-up film director creates a computer-generated actress, devises as simulated life for her, and passes her off as a real celebrity.

Hackers (1995, 107 minutes, rated PG-13). A kid is arrested for creating a computer virus and banned from using a computer until he is eighteen. Then he and some friends help the Secret Service track another virus perpetrator down.

Things to Remember When Talking with Teens About Electronic Games

- Do ask teens to demonstrate their favorite video games for you, and then try them yourself so you will know what they are experiencing.
- Do not judge what you have not experienced.
- Do be open to their opinions about video games.
- Do remind them of the moral issues of using someone else's credit card to play without express permission.
- Do address the downside of video gaming: the isolating influence it can have on younger members of the family.
- Do suggest that they assess the time they spend online or on the computer playing *Solitaire* or other games.
- Do motivate teens to assess their gaming behavior.
- Do not fail to talk about consumerism, profit, pornography, and violence in electronic games.

Activities

Activity 1: Imagining Oneself a Biblical Character

In this activity, the young people enter into the life experience of Jacob (or other biblical characters of your choice, such as David and Goliath, Ruth, or the Man Born Blind in John 9).

1. Introduce the activity to the students with this information.

    ✦ A special contribution that Saint Ignatius of Loyola made to Christian spirituality was teaching us to imagine ourselves as part of the stories in the Scriptures so that we could know God and his son Jesus better. Saint Ignatius suggests that we consider what we would have done, and what choices we would have made, if we were among the crowds depicted in the Bible, or even one of the main characters in the life of Jesus.

Media Saints and Greats

Blessed Pier Giorgio (Peter George) Frassati (1901–1925), an avid skier, mountain climber, and athlete from Torino, Italy, became a miner and practiced great charity for the poor before his early death due to polio. He lived the Christian life whether having fun, working, or helping those in need.

Venerable Maria Teresa Quevedo (1930–1950) was a thoroughly modern young woman from a prosperous family. Teresa was fearless about life; she excelled at tennis, drove too fast, and had a great sense of humor. She was devoted to Mary, the Mother of Jesus. Always generous, she wanted to dedicate her life to God; she entered the convent after high school to become a nun.

Saint Ignatius of Loyola (1491–1556) was a Spanish soldier who became a priest and founded the Jesuit Order in 1534. His spirituality is characterized by listening to the voices of the heart and spirit in silence and to imagining oneself on the scene with Jesus in the Gospels.

Media Detective

Give these interesting and fun assignments to your students so they can investigate the media. Have them report back!

- Find out how electronic video games are created.
- Find out which video games you have at home, what they are about, how they are rated, and if the stories they create are ethical and moral.
- Find out if a certain video rental chain has a policy about selling or renting violent games to children on the Internet, and if so, what it is.
- Find out more about video game awards.

✦ Video games are created and function due to our desire and ability to imagine ourselves on a hero's quest. In the best games, the hero, sometimes accompanied by friends and companions, must travel on a journey and conquer many obstacles to become a better person and reach the goal, the castle, or to return home again. Stories from the entire Book of Genesis, if not all the historical books of the Bible, could be made into video games with plenty of action and romance.

2. Reread Genesis 32:24–31 (see "Scripture Connection" at the beginning of this chapter) and other sections of Genesis about Jacob. Ask the young people to close their eyes and imagine themselves watching from behind a tent when Jacob tricked his brother or from behind a big rock as Jacob struggled with the angel. Prompt their meditation with these types of statements and questions:

- Think about where Jacob had been and where he was going.
- What will happen to his son Joseph, and how will his other sons treat Joseph in the future?
- Jacob's life had plenty of struggle, violence, romance, sin, war, and battles with evil. From a male perspective, what would you do in Jacob's place? From a female perspective, how would you have acted if you were one of two sisters married to the same man?

Conclude by making these observations:

✦ Video games can take our moral imaginations into other worlds and situations. The Scriptures invite us to do the same, as Saint Ignatius taught, so that we may understand God's story of redemption in our lives and make choices that are consistent with our faith.

Activity 2: Focus on Film

In this activity, the students view the life of Jacob, engage in a "hero's quest," and practice the art of respectful dialogue about others' opinions of Jacob's life.

1. See the movie *Jacob*, starring Matthew Modine, from The Bible Collection (1994, 94 minutes, not rated) either partially or in full. (Feel free to use another movie about a biblical hero if you do not have access to this one).

Invite the young people to talk about other hero-quest movies (*The Matrix*, the Star Wars Trilogy, *The Lion King*, *Whale Rider*, or others) and compare these with the film they have just seen. Ask these questions:

- Are all these quests noble ones? Why or why not?
- What is each character seeking?
- What is Jacob seeking, and does he find it?
- Who helps these characters fulfill their quests?

2. Break into small groups and talk about Jacob as a hero on a quest. Analyze the choices of the various characters (Laban, Esau, Rachel, Leah, Jacob's sons), the consequences of these choices for others, and how these characters create or overcome the obstacles in their lives.

3. Afterward, talk about whether Jacob does the right thing in the various situations in his life. Does he become a true hero and friend of God? Why or why not?

4. Ask the group's opinion about whether Jacob's story would make a good video game, and whether they would buy it. What elements would it need to make them buy it, and why?

5. Conclude with a prayer of praise for God's presence and action in our lives, and for the gift of creativity that respects the dignity of each person.

Activity 3: Storyboard a Bible Video Game

In this activity, the young people create a storyboard for a biblical video game.

1. After watching the story of Jacob (or David or another biblical character), have the students gather in groups of two or three.

2. Give a copy of handout 8–A, "Design a Bible Video Game," to each student so that each one can storyboard a movie sequence as if it were a video game for children from seven to ten years old. For example, Jacob starts out on a part of his life's journey, meets people and obstacles, overcomes them, and moves to the next level (sequence).

In each small group, all students can identify the obstacles, then one student can outline the story scene by scene (the director), another can write dialogue (writer), and another can sketch it (artist).

3. When the groups are finished, the students can present their game to the group and explain why they developed it as they did.

Activity 4: Electronic Games and Media Mindfulness

Bring an age-appropriate video game to the group, preferably a nonreligious one. Have the young people group around a TV or project the game onto a screen. Distribute handout 8–B, "Electronic Games and Media Mindfulness," and ask students to use this strategy as they observe the game.

Reflective Exercise

If you have access to a computer lab, gather there for this experience. If not, bring a laptop, or a large picture of a computer, to the gathering.

Create a quiet space. Display a Bible and light a candle if possible. Gather around the computer(s) in silence. Let participants know that they may of-

Cross-Curricular Connections

Mathematics and Computer Science. Research the role math plays in computer programming and applications to design video games.

Social Studies. Write a report about the role video-game culture plays in society today.

Religion. Find out how many Christian or religious video games are available. Identify the companies that make them and see if they indicate whether they are Catholic. (This might be a good time to review the difference between Catholics and other Christians.) Ask students why some Christian video games might be inconsistent with Catholic theology. (For example, the *Left Behind Games* tell a saga about the "Rapture," an apocalyptic event that does not reflect Catholic interpretation of the Scriptures.) How do religious video games compare to nonreligious games? Compare and contrast them.

Moral Theology. Ask questions such as: Do all electronic games present a reality that is good versus evil? Explain. How does the content of video games resemble or differ from the real world?

Parenting and Child Care. Have the young people research which video game systems and corresponding games they would approve, and not approve, for their child—and be able to explain why. Find out what child development experts think about video games for young children.

fer a reflection or petition if they wish. Lead this guided reflection, or one that you have written:

✦ God our Father, we thank and bless you for the gift of creation and all the marvelous communication, information, and leisure inventions that human creativity has provided for us.

○ On May 27, 1989, Pope John Paul II had this to say about the computer age in his World Communications Day statement, "The Church Must Learn to Cope with Computer Culture":

> "Let us 'trust the young.' (*Communio et Progressio*, 70) They have had the advantage of growing up with the new developments, and it will be their duty to employ these new instruments for a wider and more intense dialogue among all the diverse races and classes who share this 'shrinking globe.'
>
> It falls to them to search out ways in which the new systems of data conservation and exchange can be used to assist in promoting greater universal justice, greater respect for human rights, a healthy development for all individuals and peoples, and the freedoms essential for a fully human life.
>
> Whether we are young or old, let us rise to the challenge of new discoveries and technologies by bringing to them a moral vision rooted in our religious faith, in our respect for the human person, and our commitment to transform the world in accordance with God's plan."

Briefly pause, then continue:

✦ Let us take a few moments to reflect on these words and what they mean to us as followers of Jesus. Let's also reflect on the role of electronic media in our lives and how it influences our relationships with God and others. Are there any changes I can make to improve my relationships with God, my family, and others regarding electronic games?

Pause for a few moments, then continue:

✦ Each one of you may offer a prayer of praise or petition about the virtual world that computers offer us, or any other petitions you might have at this time.

Closing Prayer

Come and be with us, Lord, as we navigate the borders between our culture and our faith. Help us know the difference between what is real and important for faithful, joyous living and what is not. And be present to us so that the choices we make about computers, video games, and the Internet, will show us to be the Christians we say we are. Amen.

Self-Evaluation

Please fill out a copy of handout appendix 6–A, "Self-Evaluation," in this manual.

Design a Bible Video Game

Media Mindfulness and Electronic Games

(This diagram is adapted from *Believing in a Media Culture*, by Gretchen Hailer, Thomas Zanzig, and Marilyn Kielbasa [Winona, MN: Saint Mary's Press, 1996], page 38. Copyright © 1996 by Saint Mary's Press. All rights reserved.)

Chapter 9

The Internet and Media Mindfulness

Introduction

Scripture Connection

> The heavens are telling the glory of God;
>   and the firmament proclaims his
>   handiwork.
> Day to day pours forth speech,
>   and night to night declares knowledge.
> There is no speech, nor are there words;
>   their voice is not heard;
> yet their voice goes out through all the earth,
>   and their words to the end of the world.

(Psalm 19:1–4)

This psalm praises creation and God, the source of all wisdom. Today, however, we also look to the Internet for wisdom, as well as relationships, information, entertainment, and even the Scriptures. The Internet is a vast databank of information and entertainment, a gateway to the entire universe and a myriad of choices: the good, the beautiful, the unexceptional, the bad, and unfortunately, the ugly. As we apply media mindfulness to the knowledge and entertainment available on the Internet, let us pray that we will remain blameless and innocent regarding our use of the Internet. May God continue to guide us so we will always be acceptable in God's sight. Let us strive to use the Internet to build bridges of charity, peace, and social justice around the world.

Objectives

This session will enable you to accomplish the following tasks and goals:
- to acquaint students with a brief history of the Internet
- to survey various elements of the Internet
- to explore with them the positive and negative aspects of the Internet
- to help them understand their ethical and moral responsibilities as Internet users and content providers
- to consider the Church's approach to the Internet

What Is the Internet?

The Internet is a globally interconnected web of computers and computer networks linked by telephone and satellite (wireless) communications. Its other names include the World Wide Web, the Net, and the now-dated term *Information Superhighway*.

Internet content providers generally value the following:

- speed and technical excellence
- instant gratification for the user
- providing both information and entertainment
- generating commerce and profit, often through advertising
- education and communication
- appealing to users' gaming instincts
- responding to users' questions

Things to Know About the Internet

A Brief History of the Internet

It could be said that computers, the basic component of the Internet, are rooted in the abacus, which was developed between 3000 and 300 BC. The first electronic computer, using the binary system and an electronic memory, was invented by Dr. Vincent Atanasoff and Clifford E. Berry in 1939. But the modern computer age is said to have begun with the invention of the first digital computer, the Harvard Mark I, between 1939 and 1944. It was officially known as the IBM automatic sequence controlled calculator (ASCC).

In 1962, during the height of the Cold War, a Polish-born American man named Rand Paul Baran and others talked about the idea of connecting computers together. Baran and his colleagues put this system into place on a larger scale to safeguard vital government data and communicate with and within the military in case of a nuclear attack.

In 1969, the technological backbone of the network system hosted and linked several universities.

The term *Internet* was first used in 1974, and two years later Ethernet technology was developed. Ethernet is a large and diverse family of frame-based computer networking technologies for local area networks (LANs), enabling coaxial cable carrying multiple channels to move information at high speed. The Domain Name System (DNS) was created in 1983 to allow computer users to use names such as *smp.org* rather than lengthy address numbers. In 1985 the National Science Foundation began using the T1 lines it developed that enabled many people to use the Internet at once. A hypertext system was first used in 1990; this system allows the use of hyperlinks. Until 1992, use of the Internet was reserved for the U.S. Department of Defense and data-driven academic research.

Between 1992 and 1993, the World Wide Web was made publicly available to everyone. The Internet Society was chartered that same year to provide leadership around Internet issues and to act as an international organization for global cooperation and coordination. E-mail was actually created prior to the Internet because originally it allowed people who were sharing time on a mainframe computers to communicate with one another. E-mail quickly became a part of people's daily lives as the Internet became publicly available.

The Internet and Communication

The term *cyberspace* was popularized by William Gibson in his 1984 futuristic "cyberpunk" techno novel, *Neuromancer*. The term is often used to refer to objects and identities that exist largely within the computing network itself. Cyberspace is there, but you cannot touch it or see it.

The Internet has opened a whole new way for people to communicate with one another. For the youngest generation, the Internet is a completely normal mode of communication. People use e-groups, online communities that post information and hold conversations about their interests.

They post blogs (Web logs), which can be dedicated to different topics or can function as online journals. It seems the first blog surfaced around 1994, but personal blogs now flood the Internet. Blogging gives a voice to anyone who has access to the Internet and takes the time to write about his or her opinions, life stories, hobbies, work, and so forth. Blogs are probably the single largest threat to professional journalism because anyone on the ground where events are happening can take digital photos, post them, and write a personal view of an event, or of political, economic, or religious policies and personages.

Though everyone is free to communicate as he or she sees fit, whether in a national newspaper or a personal blog, that freedom is balanced by responsibility. Truth, human dignity, service, respect, civility, and charity are the hallmarks of communication that builds relationships and contributes to peacemaking.

The Internet and Culture

When we communicate from person to person via the Internet, relationships are formed. We communicate about things that are important to us; therefore the content of our communication reflects our values, what we think is important and why. When these values are authentic and human, a culture is born. Genuine culture always has a spiritual dimension.

The Internet provides much good to the world culture. For many people in the United States, checking e-mail once or twice a day is as natural as brushing one's teeth. Americans have learned to think and write in bytes and even in emotion symbols (such as ☺), which signifies the emergence of new styles of relating. Web sites provide information, offer online shopping, recruit followers for political candidates and issues, facilitate class reunions and retreats, and even provide Mass times for travelers. Not only is the Internet the largest encyclopedia in history, but it has also helped make the world a global marketplace as well.

These new ways of living and behaving, and of ordering one's priorities, signify that a new culture has emerged, evolving with its own values and ways of communicating.

The Internet in Times of Crisis

In times of tragedy and need—such the months following September 11, 2001, the tsunami of Christmas 2004, and Hurricanes Katrina and Rita in 2005—the Internet helped families find one another and keep in touch, and provided donation channels to aid organizations.

The Internet, with its e-mail, Web sites, forums, and blogs, can let the world know what's going on, from natural disasters to local politics to social and cultural movements accelerated by the Web.

The Internet and Democracy

Now widely available, Internet communication is used for commentary and opinion sharing and shaping, thus making it one of the most democratizing technologies of all time. News and views no longer belong only to the dominant multinational media corporations. Although professional news outlets may claim objectivity in news reporting, a blogger has the advantage of immediacy when a drug deal, car accident, or more major event plays out in his or her neighborhood. But all news gathering, reporting, and experiencing is told from some point of view, so that news is rarely, if ever, objective. This is why an attitude of inquiry is necessary in today's media world.

Some people have constant access to the Internet while others have none: hence the gap between the information rich and the information poor, called the digital divide. The Internet has multiplied the number of voices, but the entire world does not have access to it—yet.

Navigating the Minefield

The Internet is a garden, but it is also a minefield and every other kind of terrain in between. Those who provide Internet content are called to respect the human person, but as in other areas of communication, they do not always do so. Because profit drives the Internet as it does other media, the Internet provides opportunities for people to exploit and otherwise offend the dignity of other people.

The principles of Catholic social teaching provide Christians with guidance in their use of the Internet (see appendix 2). With the Internet, as with other modes of communication, the dignity of each person should set the standard for any ethical issues involved.

Some critics focus on moral issues such as obvious obscenities and lack of civility in Internet communication and miss the problems of a market economy and democracy that allows content providers to offer them. Freedom of speech requires consumers to be discerning and responsible because there are few standards that people can agree on to regulate media and to preserve the public's right to the air waves or cyberspace. The Internet is another way that people can consume pornography or gamble, both of which can be addictive. Media mindfulness provides the skills that can help us choose wisely and create media that respects the dignity of the human person above all.

For Internet users, critical judgment (asking questions about Internet content, the artistic representation, and so on) is vital to making ethical and moral decisions that are right, good, and just regarding the use of this amazing technology. We are also called to remember our human weaknesses. Some Internet users prey on these weaknesses as well as on vulnerable people for profit through the use of pornography, gambling, and gaming to the exclusion of familial, social, religious, and community responsibilities.

The Internet and Adolescent Moral Development

Because the frontal cortex of the young person's brain is not completely developed, teens often fail to think about the consequences of their behavior, or they think they are invincible and nothing bad will ever happen to them. Some young people are highly skilled programmers and are able to hack into sensitive computer systems or create viruses that could have serious consequences for a company, a bank, a laboratory, or the government. Some do it because they can, not because they have thought out the results of their actions. This phenomenon is called developmental compression. Kids are getting "older" in proficiency and skill at a younger age, and they do not have the maturity to realize the consequences of their actions.

Misuse of the Internet and Other Digital Technologies

A common storyline that appears in films such as *The Perfect Man* (2005, 100 minutes, rated PG-13) and *Hackers* (1995, 107 minutes, rated PG-13) is the trouble kids cause for themselves and others when they use technology for harm rather than good. By using the Ten Commandments and themes of Catholic social teaching as a framework (see appendix 2), it is easy to understand why the following misuses of the Internet (and other devices) are wrong, often illegal, and objectively sinful. All of the following actions are irresponsible misuses of personal freedom and dignity because they offend and infringe upon the rights and dignity of others:

- photographing people without their permission or inappropriately and then sharing the photo via phone, e-mail, or Web site
- creating or knowingly sending a virus via e-mail
- initiating or sharing gossip about others (even if supposedly true) via e-mail or text messaging

- spending so much time on the Internet and text messaging that one's family relationships, school, and church and charitable activities are negatively impacted
- sharing one's own personal information, or that of others, online
- agreeing to meet in person anyone met online
- hacking into anyone's account, or into any entity that is not one's own
- stealing or selling identities or credit card information, or "phishing" to obtain this information
- stealing or buying someone else's term or thesis papers and passing them off as one's own, or using any technology to cheat at school or in other settings
- downloading and sharing music, movies, and other copyrighted material instead of purchasing them

Pornography

Pornography is an example of the more sinful side of the Internet, all the more so because it is easily accessed by people of all ages. Pornography is free and downloadable, and can be accessed by file-sharing and through spam (unsolicited junk mail).

In 2003, Rep. Henry A. Waxman (D-California) addressed the U.S. Congress about the need to close the online generational divide and raise children safely in the digital age:

> There's a new technology that's widely available that allows teenagers to download X-rated videos directly into their home computers.
>
> The most popular of these programs is Kazaa, which has been downloaded nearly 200 million times. Other popular programs include Morpheus, BearShare, and Grokster. At any given time, there are millions of teenagers between the ages of 12 and 18 using these programs.
>
> Most adults I talk with don't know about these programs. But if they do, all they know is that the entertainment industry doesn't like

them because they threaten their copyrights.

> . . . Whenever a tech-savvy teenager logs on to programs like Kazaa, he or she has access to millions of hard-core pornographic files.
>
> Parents may think that by installing parental control software programs like Net Nanny or Cyber Patrol, they can protect their children from this pornography. But our investigation also found that while these programs might work to keep kids from pornography on the World Wide Web, they do not work in the same way for file-sharing programs. There are some programs that can be configured—after some effort—to block access to all file-sharing programs. But there's really nothing that works effectively in filtering out pornographic files once a child has access to these programs. As legislators, we can try to pass laws. But I'm not sure there's a legislative solution available for this problem. In this case, parental awareness and parental involvement matter more than legislation. Parents need to better understand these file-sharing programs and know if their kids are using them. Parents need to talk to their children about what to do when they come across this pornography. ("Hearing on Stumbling into Smut," March 13, 2003)

Tips for Talking with Teens About Pornography and the Internet

The best way to counter pornography is to talk to kids and keep talking to them. Create a relationship where conversations about both unimportant things and vital, important things are normal. In addition, educate and form children and teens to an understanding of the body and the gift of sexuality. Share some of the following information about pornography with teens:

- pornography, including snuff films, is addictive.
- pornography debases men and women because it focuses only on body parts and functions, not on the whole person. It teaches people to use

others as sex objects rather than to form real relationships.

- Pornography debases the women and men who are photographed or filmed. These people are sometimes lured into this type of film and then trapped once they understand fully what they have gotten into.
- Pornography is a deterrent to lasting, meaningful relationships and to raising a healthy family.
- We all have latent curiosity about sexuality; this is a good thing. Sex should not be separated from its purpose within marriage, which is to contribute to the mutual growth in holiness of the husband and wife and to procreate. If we do not view sexuality in its role to fulfill our true nature as human beings, we will not possess a balanced sexuality and a wholesome life.
- Pornography leads to crimes against the most vulnerable people in our society, especially when it is paired with violence. These crimes include domestic abuse, child abuse, rape, pedophilia, kidnapping, and murder.
- If a person's ideas about sexuality are balanced, then he or she can say no when presented with pornography, and will not go looking for it.
- Pornography is a billion-dollar industry. By using porn and becoming addicted to it, we are furthering the debasement of ourselves as well as of the men and women who produce it, act in it, and consume it.
- Pornographers exploit the weaknesses of human persons; there is nothing transcendent or life-giving about pornography.

Talking About Pornography with Parents

Provide parents and caregivers with the latest information about pornography so they can educate children and create fewer opportunities for access to it. This is some of the information you will want to share if you have a group of parents and caregivers to address on this topic:

- Review the ideas in "Tips for Talking with Teens About Pornography and the Internet."

- Encourage parents to move computers, televisions, and DVD players out of kids' bedrooms and into common areas, and explain the reason to their kids. Monitor their peer-to-peer sites.
- Present a contract for both parents and teens to sign that stipulates that they will avoid inappropriate chat rooms, surfing for pornography, and revealing important personal information to anyone they do not know.
- Help parents craft rules for Internet use based on rewards and loss of privileges.
- Suggest that parents check teens' bedrooms for other forms of pornography.
- Encourage parents to install software on all their computers that will filter out pornographic spam—even if there are only adults in the house.
- Study and share with parents the Children's Online Privacy Protection Act of 1998, which went into effect in 2000.
- Encourage parents to stay up to date with technology.
- Check telephone bills for unusual charges. Phone pornography already exists; cell phones can also receive video porn.

How to Evaluate Information on the Internet

The Internet is the largest databank of information in the world. It is a good idea, however, to evaluate the information mindfully and critically. Use these questions to help young people evaluate Internet sites:

- What is the URL (Uniform Resource Locator)? Do you recognize it?
- What is the domain name? Is the extension ".edu," ".gov," or another domain you recognize and can verify? Is it an organization, a company, a foundation, a school, or an individual?
- Who is the author of the information? Can you verify the author's credentials through the domain and URL?

- Does the information respond to your inquiry? Does it seem reasonable? Be sure to verify the information and facts from at least one other source.
- If the site identifies itself as Catholic, apply these same criteria to determine the authenticity of the source and content.

The Church and the Internet

In 2002, Pope John Paul II called the Internet "a window on the world." (cf. World Communications Day message) It is interesting to hear the Church speak through the auspices of its Pontifical Council for Social Communication's 2002 document *The Church and Internet*. It begins:

The Church's interest in the Internet is a particular expression of her longstanding interest in the media of social communication. Seeing the media as an outcome of the historical scientific process by which humankind "advances further and further in the discovery of the resources and values contained in the whole of creation", the Church often has declared her conviction that they are, in the words of the Second Vatican Council, "marvelous technical inventions" that already do much to meet human needs and may yet do even more. (No. 1)

The document continues to express praise for all the possibilities the Internet provides, as well as insight into the following areas.

- The Internet contributes to globalization in both positive and negative ways: on the one hand, it has increased communications between cultures, but on the other hand, some perceive globalization to threaten their social norms and cultural points of reference. (No. 4)
- The Internet's news reporting is immediate but not always complete. (Nos. 6, 7, and 12)
- The Internet contributes to democracy and social justice by giving more people the op-

portunity to voice their opinions. (No. 12)
- The Internet creates a digital divide: not everyone has access to it. (Nos. 10 and 17)
- We are called to be mindful about the ways the Internet gives us to see the world and ourselves. (No. 1)

The Vatican documents cover a range of moral and ethical communication concerns, from personal Internet behavior to freedom and responsibility in the social and global spheres by individuals, companies, groups, and governments.

Some practical advice to young people comes from *The Church and Internet*:

Young people, as has often been said, are the future of society and the Church. Good use of the Internet can help prepare them for their responsibilities in both. But this will not happen automatically. The Internet is not merely a medium of entertainment and consumer gratification. It is a tool for accomplishing useful work, and the young must learn to see it and use it as such. In cyberspace, at least as much as anywhere else, they may be called on to go against the tide, practice counter-culturalism, and even suffer persecution for the sake of what is true and good. (No. 11)

Finally, then, we would suggest some virtues that need to be cultivated by everyone who wants to make good use of the Internet; their exercise should be based upon and guided by a realistic appraisal of its contents.

Prudence is necessary in order clearly to see the implications—the potential for good and evil—in this new medium and to respond creatively to its challenges and opportunities.

Justice is needed, especially justice in working to close the digital divide—the gap between the information-rich and the information-poor in today's world. This requires a commitment to the international common good, no less than the "globalization of solidarity."

Fortitude, courage, is necessary. This means standing up for truth in the face of religious and moral relativism, for altruism and generosity in the face of individualistic consumerism, for decency in the face of sensuality and sin.

And temperance is needed—a selfdisciplined approach to this remarkable technological instrument, the Internet, so as to use it wisely and only for good. (No. 12)

Movies About the Internet

Use clips from these films to illustrate a point or begin a conversation, or show an entire film to your group and analyze it together.

The Net (1995, 114 minutes, rated PG-13). Angela is a computer whiz who gets embroiled in a computer conspiracy.

You've Got Mail (1998, 119 minutes, rated PG). A man and woman begin an anonymous online relationship without realizing they are rivals in real life: he wants to buy the land where her small bookstore is located.

Hackers (1995, 107 minutes, rated PG-13). A kid is arrested for creating an Internet virus and banned from using a computer until he is eighteen. Then he and some friends discover that a terrible new virus is to be released and they help the Secret Service track down the perpetrator.

The Perfect Man (2005, 100 minutes, rated PG). A teenage girl, tired of moving from place to place with her single mom and sister, pretends to be a man who is interested in her mom and sends her e-mail, notes, and gifts. When the virtual relationship is successful, things get complicated.

Characteristics of Internet Communication

- is powerful because of the knowledge it provides
- is attractive and enticing
- informs with great speed

- reaches around the world
- is anonymous
- is commercially driven

Things to Remember When Talking with Teens About the Internet

- Do remember that young people most certainly know more than you do about Web technology and content.
- Do not assume that they are involved in dangerous, illegal, or immoral activities online.
- Do realize that they probably spend too much time instant messaging or in chat rooms, but do not assume that they spend too much time online.
- Do ask them about their online activities.
- Do not judge them for their online activities.
- Do motivate them to evaluate their online behavior.
- Do be creative about ways to change their online behavior or to channel it productively, such as teaching older relatives how to use the Internet, and so on.
- Do talk about hacking; creating and spreading online viruses; copying papers, essays, and exams; and other morally wrong (and probably illegal) activities and their consequences.
- Do promote respectful, community-building, civil online etiquette.

Media Saints and Greats

Saint Isidore of Seville (560–636), a Spanish archbishop, wrote a history of the world and compiled an encyclopedia or *summa* of universal knowledge, a version of what we would now call an information databank.

Blessed James Alberione, SSP (1884–1971) was an Italian priest who founded the Society of Saint Paul and Daughters of Saint Paul to communicate the Good News of the Gospel using all the means of communication available.

Media Detective

Give these interesting and fun assignments to your students so they can investigate the media. Have them report back!

- Find out what an abacus is and how to use one.
- Find out who invented the Harvard Mark I computer and identify its characteristics.
- Find out the Pope's e-mail address and send him a greeting or ask him a question.
- Find out how many Web sites there are today compared to ten years ago.
- Find out about the contracts for Internet use that kids make with their parents or caregivers and that parents can make with the kids.
- Find out if any countries forbid, limit, censor, or track the Internet use of its citizens, and to what extent and why.
- Find out how many documents the Vatican has issued on the Internet and list five of their titles.
- Find out what awards are given for Internet excellence.

Activities

Activity 1: Imagining "Web World!"

This activity provides the young people with a visualization of what a Web-connected world looks like.

1. Tear out full-page ads for companies and services from magazines or newspapers; try to find some from other countries. Get a large ball of yarn and a globe or large map.

2. Gather the group and have them sit in an irregular circle.

3. Give each person an ad and ask them what service or item is being sold or promoted, and whether it offers a Web address.

4. Now hold the end of the yarn and start passing the ball from one person to another in a zigzag fashion, each person keeping hold of the yarn as he or she throws the ball away. The ball of yarn should end up with you.

5. Talk about how the crisscrossing of the yarn is a visual way of imagining the invisible wires that connect us through cable or satellite. Each person represents a computer somewhere in the world that is providing information or selling items for a company, organization, or a government.

6. Talk about how these lines of communication cut across borders, and can be used for others things such as news, e-mail, and entertainment. Talk about access in underdeveloped countries and how some people can, for example, can order goods and services with credit cards and how some cannot.

7. Ask them how they think a responsible Christian and citizen conducts business in a wired—or wireless—world. Ask the students how they would act if they moved to Singapore where the government censors advertising on the Internet (as well as blogs).

Activity 2: Designing a Web Site

This activity gives the young people the opportunity to design a Web site.

Using handout 9–A, "Designing a Web Site," have the young people develop a Web page that would work for their school, parish, or youth group. Discuss their results.

Activity 3: Character Analysis

This activity provides a scriptural lens for young people to analyze characters in movies about the Internet.

1. With the students, choose from the "Movies About the Internet" list which movies to see, either partially or in full. Write the name of several key characters from the films on separate index cards.

2. Read this verse (or another Scripture verse) aloud to the young people and then post it in a visible spot. "When I was a child, I spoke like a child, I thought like a child, I reasoned like a child; when I became an adult, I put an end to childish ways" (1 Cor. 13:11). Invite students to use the verse as a lens through which you view the films and the characters.

3. Pass out the index cards, one per person.

4. After watching the movies, break into small groups and talk about how the Scripture quotation applies to the various characters. If you use only clips, take extra time with these characters if applicable:
- The Cereal Killer, Dade, and Kate, in *Hackers*
- Angela, in *The Net*
- Joe and Kathleen, in *You've Got Mail*
- Holly, in *The Perfect Man*

5. Gather together in the large group again and ask each small group to share one point that emerged from their conversation.

Activity 4: Media Mindfulness and the Internet

This activity applies the strategy of media mindfulness to the Internet.

Handout 9–B, "The Internet and Media Mindfulness," can be used when evaluating any Web site or use of the Internet in general.

Reflective Exercise

In preparation for this reflective exercise, make a 5- to 7-minute PowerPoint prayer using stock nature photos found in clip art or other sources (or photos the young people take), put to original music—or music that is in the public domain—and the words from the Psalms or other scriptures that reflect on God's glory and creation.

Create a quiet space. In silence, show the Power-Point. End the prayer experience by reciting or singing a psalm of praise together for all the marvelous technologies that help people in the world communicate. If rights are all clear, post this PowerPoint on the Web so others can play and pray it as well.

Closing Prayer

Lord God, we bless and thank you for your gift of creation, and for the talents you have given your people to invent such marvelous technologies that help us communicate your love in justice and peace. May we be aware of your presence in cyberspace and respect the dignity of all who use the Internet, especially the lonely, the infirm, and those who seek meaning in their lives. Grant us the grace to be people of peace. We ask this through Christ our Lord. Amen.

Self-Evaluation

Please fill out a copy of handout appendix 6–A, "Self-Evaluation," in this manual.

Cross-Curricular Connections

Mathematics. Explore the role of discrete mathematics in computers and the Internet.

History. Research the role of the fax machine in informing the world about the Tiananmen Square protests in Beijing in 1989, and compare that role with the role bloggers have played in a more recent world event. Why is free speech important?

Theology. Some have suggested that Saint Isidore of Seville should be named the patron saint of the Internet; others have suggested Blessed James Alberione as patron of all the media once he is canonized. Have students research both of these candidates, as well as others they discover, and vote on their choice, noting the reasons for the choice.

Literature. Search the Web for a commentary on one of the books on your required reading list. Analyze the site and the commentary itself as part of your report on the book.

Designing a Web Site

Working alone or with another person, fill out this template.

Name of the site:

_____

_____

_____

Purpose of the site:

_____

_____

_____

Sponsoring organization:

_____

_____

_____

Kinds of content to achieve the purpose:

- information for parents
- information for teens
- news
- calendar
- contacts
- links

Media Mindfulness and the Internet

1. What is going on?

What am I seeing? hearing? reading?

2. What is really going on?

Who sponsors this site? What is its purpose? How do the contents respect human dignity?

3. What difference does it make?

What Christian values, morals, or social issues are supported or ignored in this Web site?

4. What difference can I make?

What kind of personal and group response seems appropriate?

Media Mindfulness and the Internet

(This diagram is adapted from *Believing in a Media Culture*, by Gretchen Hailer, Thomas Zanzig, and Marilyn Kielbasa [Winona, MN: Saint Mary's Press, 1996], p. 38. Copyright © 1996 by Saint Mary's Press. All rights reserved.)

Chapter 10

The Theology and Spirituality of Communication

Introduction

Scripture Connection

> There was a man sent from God, whose name was John. He came as a witness to testify to the light, so that all might believe through him. He himself was not the light, but he came to testify to the light. The true light, which enlightens everyone, was coming into the world.
>
> He was in the world, and the world came into being through him; yet, the world did not know him. He came to what was his own, and his own people did not accept him. But to all who received him, who believed in his name, he gave power to become children of God, who were born, not of blood or of the will of the flesh or of the will of man, but of God.
>
> And the Word became flesh and lived among us, and we have seen his glory, the glory as of a father's only son, full of grace and truth. (John testified to him and cried out, "This was he of whom I said, 'He who comes after me ranks ahead of me because he was before me.'") From his fullness we have all received, grace upon grace. The law indeed was given through Moses; grace and truth came through Jesus Christ. No one has ever seen God. It is God the only Son, who is close to the Father's heart, who has made him known. (John 1:6–18)

Though modern technology has changed and expanded the ways people can communicate with one another, the Christian faith has always been one based on communication and relationship, whether that be in the Trinity itself, in the Scriptures (the word of God), in the Eucharist, in the study of theology, or in evangelization. As a Church community, we share our values through communication in order to be the Body of Christ in the world, creating a culture of Gospel values.

Session Objectives

This session will enable you to accomplish the following tasks and goals:
- to explore the theology and spirituality of communication
- to consider the Church and the theology and spirituality of communication
- to look at the Church and communication since Vatican II
- to integrate the theology and spirituality of communication into media mindfulness

What Is the Theology of Communication?

The theology of communication is an effort to understand God's self-communication as Father, Son, and Spirit to humanity, and our response to God's gift. From this theological premise, we seek to understand this continual gift of God's self-communication through the Scriptures, the Church, the community of believers, liturgy, the sacraments, the community, ministry and service, human events, the signs of the times, and the entire culture in which we live, breathe, move, and have our being.

What Is Spirituality?

"Spirituality is a life guided by the Holy Spirit, lived out within the community of believers, and characterized by faith, hope, love, and service." (The Catholic Faith Handbook for Youth [CFH], p. 425)

Media mindful educators often value the following:

- all forms of communication in the Church and world
- an incarnational approach to mediated communication—that is, being in love with the world as it is today
- media storytelling where the seeds of the Gospels can be found
- pastoral planning for communication so that it can be integrated into all areas of Church life to facilitate the Church's mission in the world
- human dignity
- sacramentality
- an integrated approach to contemplation and action

Things to Know About the Theology and Spirituality of Communication

The History of the Theology and Spirituality of Communication

Because the Trinity is infinite and is a community of love, it is possible to say there never was a beginning to the "theology and spirituality of communication," because loving communication is God. God is loving communication.

In time, however, a theology of communication began when ". . . the earth was a formless void and darkness covered the face of the deep, while a wind from God swept over the face of the waters. Then God said, 'Let there be light'; and there was light" (Genesis 1:2–3). Throughout the Old Testament, the covenant relationship that God had with God's people, Israel, was based on the Ten Commandments, a specific code given by God to the people and reinforced through the preaching of the prophets. The people promised to remain faithful, so as to be in relationship.

Jesus himself was all about relationships—with his Father, his disciples, the people he met—so much so that when he suffered, died, and rose from the dead, a small Christian community, or culture, had been formed based on the values he had preached. His own disciples received the Holy Spirit to share the message with Jews and Gentiles.

The continuity of the Catholic Church through history is due in great part to the words of missionaries, the written Old and New Testaments, the preservation of Church writings, and the writings of the doctors of the Church and saints. Communication has allowed the Catholic Church to be a global Church.

As previous chapters have recounted, the twentieth century saw a rapid growth of new communication styles, powered by commerce rather than faith. Though the written and spoken forms may have been taken for granted in previous centuries, "communication" itself became an increasingly important issue in the contemporary Church. Although the earlier twentieth-century documents acknowledge that motion pictures, then radio and television, are gifts of God, they are very concerned with prohibitions, cautions, and the evil these means can cause in people's souls.

Vatican II's 1963 *Decree on the Means of Social Communication (Inter Mirifica)* focused exclusively on mass media or means of social communication. Vatican II commissioned a deeper study of the theology of communication that resulted in the 1971 document *The Pastoral Instruction for the Application of the Decree of the Second Vatican Council on The Means of Social Communication (Communio et Progressio)*. This document laid a foundation for a theology of communication. It calls Christ "the perfect communicator" (no. 11) and shows that the Eucharist leads to communion, that is, "communio" and community (no. 11).

The Trinity

Saint Anselm called theology "faith seeking understanding." The Trinity is at the core of any theology. Fr. Bernard R. Bonnot explains this concept:

> Contemporary theologians understand the Trinity's inner life as self-communicating love, a dynamic and intimate sharing among persons. The technical term for this is *communio*. This approach provides promising grounds for considering communications a core ministry, one at the heart of what the Church is all about. In addition, Trinity stands as source, model, and goal of all godly and Christian communication.
>
> Reflection on Trinity manifests how central communications is to our life as Church. ("Basics in Communications Theology")

As pastoral ministers and teachers, we can contemplate the *communio* of the Trinity, this wonderful community of love that gives value to all authentic human communication. We can imitate this communication by allowing love to be the content and the process of our personal bonds with others. We can pastorally plan for authentic communication, as it is essential to all pastoral activity. We can seek to build bridges to enable communication between faith and culture—not only to plant seeds of the Gospel in culture, but to find the seeds that are already there.

The Incarnation

The Pastoral Constitution of the Church in the Modern World (Gaudium et Spes) from Vatican II reminds us that the matters of this world are important:

> The joys and the hopes, the griefs and the anxieties of the men of this age, especially those who are poor or in any way afflicted, these are the joys and hopes, the griefs and anxieties of the followers of Christ. Indeed, nothing genuinely human fails to raise an echo in their hearts. For theirs is a community composed of men. United in Christ, they are led by the Holy Spirit in their journey to the Kingdom of their Father and they have welcomed the news of salvation which is meant for every man. That is why this community realizes that it is truly linked with mankind and its history by the deepest of bonds. (No. 1)

The Catholic Church has a sacramental worldview—meaning that God's presence can be found in all of creation. The belief that the world matters and that God can be found in it and communicates to us through it, form the bases for the two lenses in media mindfulness—the first lens offering Gospel values in our assessment of media in all forms, and the second lens inviting us to find the seeds of the Gospel in media, reflect on them, and respond to them through action.

The Themes of Catholic Social Teaching

Catholic social teaching is based on respect for human dignity, the reality that the needs of all God's people are equal to our own, and the truth that we are not separate units, but a body for whom we have responsibility.

Pope John Paul II wrote an apostolic letter in January 2001 to close the twentieth century and welcome the twenty-first. What is so remarkable about this document is that it is permeated with Trinitarian theology, hence, a theology and spirituality of communion and communication. Pope John Paul II wrote:

> We need *to promote a spirituality of communion,* making it the guiding principle of education wherever individuals and Christians are formed, wherever ministers of the altar, consecrated persons, and pastoral workers are trained, wherever families and communities are being built up. A spirituality of communion indicates above all the heart's contemplation of the mystery of the Trinity dwelling in us, and whose light we must also be able to see shining on the face of the brothers and sisters around us. A spirituality of communion also means an ability to think of our brothers and sisters in faith within the profound unity of the Mystical Body, and therefore as "those who are a part of me." This makes us able to share their joys and sufferings, to sense their desires and attend to their needs, to offer them deep and genuine friendship. A spirituality of communion implies also the ability to see what is positive in others, to welcome it and prize it as a gift from God: not only as a gift for the brother or sister who has received it directly, but also as a "gift for me." A spirituality of communion means, finally, to know how to "make room" for our brothers and sisters, bearing "each other's burdens" (Gal. 6:2) and resisting the selfish temptations which constantly beset us and provoke competition, careerism, distrust and jealousy. Let us have no illusions: unless we follow this spiritual path, external structures of communion will serve very little purpose. They would become mechanisms without a soul, "masks" of communion rather than its means of expression and growth. ("Apostolic Letter *Novo Millennio Ineunte*," no. 43)

Those who practice media mindfulness use Catholic social teaching principles in addition to the Ten Commandments for guidance, because in our interconnected world, media informs us about situations locally and globally, and because the way we use communication tools can make a difference for people thousands of miles away.

A Spirituality of Communication

"Spirituality is a life guided by the Holy Spirit, lived out within the community of believers, and characterized by faith, hope, love, and service" (*CFH*, p. 425). Everything, then, contributes to the unfolding of our lives in the Spirit, and everything has a way of nurturing it. Because as Catholic Christians we believe that all human experience can lead us to God in some way or another, the communications media can be part of a vital spirituality.

To love the world the way it is—this is an Incarnational approach to life and culture, and is lived as the integration of faith and everyday reality. A paraphrase of John 3:17 highlights this attitude: "Indeed, God did not send the Son into the culture to condemn the culture, but in order that the culture might be saved through him." To be in love with the world today is the essential attitude for living the spiritual life in a mediated world.

A spirituality of media and communication are supported by a vibrant sacramental life, centered in the liturgy. Sacraments are encounters with Jesus and mediations of God's grace, which always brings us into communion with God and others. This desire—to live a spirituality for today—can be enhanced by the media we choose to experience, and by authentic spiritual practices that integrate faith and life on a daily basis.

- News, whatever its vehicle of dissemination, can make us alive to both the tragic and the tremendous. We can "pray" the news and make it part of our everyday spiritual practice.
- Television can hourly, daily, weekly bring us continuous stories of life in ways that make us laugh, cry, or both. These stories can move us to gratitude for the many ways that God has graced human experience.
- Movies have a way of beckoning us into the big picture in more ways than one. They can bring us to places we could never visit and can tell stories that would otherwise remain untold.
- Cell phones keep our loved ones close. They can also warn others of dangers or provide help for those in need.
- TV and radio talk shows can bring us other perspectives than our own and enable us to enter into meaningful dialogue with others.
- Internet chat rooms can do the same, provided, of course, that we realize the fact that some people may not be who they seem to be.
- Video games can help us build collaborative worlds rather than exterminating those who are different from us.

So, in fact, our preferred genres of any medium can make us better people if we use proper discernment when choosing and using them.

The Church and Communication in the United States Since Vatican II

Characterizing the Church in the United States, Sr. Elizabeth Thoman, CHM, describes its approach to a theology of communication as a somewhat unbalanced three-legged stool made up of preaching, public relations, and prophecy.

She believes that the release of *Inter Mirifica* in 1963 led catechists, Catholic school teachers, clergy, and others to begin using audiovisuals to spread the Christian message. This was the age of preaching and using the *media as instruments,* and it continues today.

Communio et Progressio was published in 1971, and it inspired dioceses to open communications offices and allow their directors to be in contact with secular society and media. She calls this the Saint Paul method because it tries to explain the Church to the world and to engage society and culture in dialogue. The Saint Paul method started off well in the United States but continues today only on a limited scale.

Then, in 1991, *Aetatis Novae* was issued, following closely upon Pope John Paul II's *Mission of the Redeemer (Redemptoris Missio),* no. 37c. *Aetatis Novae* is a prophetic document that asked the Church to be informed, to reflect *on* the culture created by communications media, and to specifically include media education in diocesan pastoral plans for communication (no. 24d) to form Catholics and people of good will to engage critically and responsibly in the media culture—as audience and as producers of media.

At the end of the twentieth century and the beginning of the twenty-first, Sister Thoman is convinced we are in the third phase, the age of *prophetic communications*, a perfect time and opportunity for the Church to be a leader in media literacy education and faith formation. This type of leadership from the Church enables people to engage the culture for the sake of the Gospel. Sister Thoman thinks the stool is still wobbly because the prophetic leg continues to call for implementation; the lack of this dimension explains why people are confused about media. Many either ignore them or go to extremes and react rather than respond. Good pastoral ministry practices will help people develop the skills they need to navigate with relevance the mediated culture in which we live. The creative industries are growing faster than any other. It is our responsibility as pastoral ministers to integrate media mindfulness and faith formation so we can influence the culture that communications media continues to create.

Movies About the Theology and Spirituality of Communications

Use clips from these films to illustrate a point or begin a conversation, or your group could see an entire movie and analyze it together.

Simon Birch (1998, 113 minutes, rated PG). This feature film is about a young boy, born with severe physical handicaps, who shows an awareness of God, God's call for him, and what God means to him by giving his life for others.

Entertaining Angels (1996, 112 minutes, rated PG-13). This movie tells the story of the Catholic social activist Dorothy Day, who began the Catholic Worker Movement. Especially relevant is the scene towards the end, when Dorothy prays in anger and frustration in church.

Characteristics of a Theology and Spirituality of Communication

- enlivens ministries
- creates community and culture
- encourages personal and communal growth
- is based on the principles of Catholic social teaching
- is holistic
- is spirit-led
- embraces head, heart, and hands
- nurtures spirit, body, and soul
- is sacramental
- is incarnational, in love with the world today

Things to Remember When Talking with Teens About a Theology and Spirituality of Communication

- Do keep the presentation simple. Replace difficult terminology with words and phrases young people are more familiar with.
- Do use visuals and examples that are meaningful to the group whenever possible.
- Do remember that you probably know more than young people about this area, so invite them to join you on the journey of "faith seeking understanding" through communication.
- Do encourage them to honor and nurture their own spirituality.
- Do not equate spirituality with piety or devotionalism.
- Do help them realize the need for a balance between contemplation and action.
- Do not disparage media as a place where it is difficult to find God.
- Do encourage them to search for God and the seeds of the gospel in whatever media they choose.

Media Detective

Give these interesting and fun assignments to your students so they can investigate the intersection of media, theology, and spirituality. Have them report back!

- Find out what World Communications Day is, and when and how is it observed in the United States and Canada, in your diocese, and in your parish.
- Find out the subjects of the Pontifical Messages for World Communications Day since the first one in 1967 and list ten.
- Find out how the Greeks treated Saint Paul when he spoke to them in Athens, as recounted in Acts 17.
- Find out what a papal bull is. Find the difference between an encyclical, apostolic letter, pastoral instruction, decree, and apostolic exhortation.
- Find out which recent Pope was an actor and playwright.
- Find five contemporary celebrities who are Catholic Christians.

Activities

Activity 1: Considering Divine Communication

In this activity, the young people take a look at communication in the Bible.

1. Read the story of the Tower of Babel, in Genesis 11:1–9, and invite reactions or comments from the group about the story.

2. Then read Acts 2 and invite reactions and comments to that story. Next compare and contrast both passages from these angles:
- the image of God
- communication
- how God's communication with people leads to understanding
- how the people who want to be like or compete with God ultimately are not able to communicate

Activity 2: Theology of Communication in Action

Divide the group into pairs. Assign each pair one of the following research topics. Give them the option to present the information creatively, for example as a PowerPoint presentation or as a booklet made of pages printed from Web sites.

- Research how many religious congregations have some kind of media communications as their principal mission or apostolate in the Church around the world. Describe the apostolate or ministry of the congregations, their spiritual charisms, the names of the congregations, years founded, name(s) of the founder(s), country or countries where the congregations are located, and other interesting information. Try to obtain some vocational information from the religious orders with a clear statement of the congregation's mission.
- Research the media activities of the Vatican: newspaper, radio, television, Internet, and so on.

Media Saints and Greats

Saint Paul (c. AD 3–AD 67) is the patron saint of journalists, evangelists, missionaries, newspaper editorial staffs, public relations personnel, reporters, and writers. He was a communicator, whether he walked or went by ship from one place to another, whether he spoke, preached, or wrote. Many say that if Saint Paul were alive today, he would use all means of communication to proclaim the love of Christ the world over.

Marshall McLuhan (1911–1980) was a Canadian philosopher, academic, and theorist of communication who created the groundwork for media literacy education and media mindfulness. He is considered the "patron saint" of *Wired* magazine.

Blessed Mother Teresa of Calcutta (1910–1997) founded the Missionaries of Charity. She always taught that "Every time you smile at someone, it is an action of love, a gift to that person, a beautiful thing."

Archbishop Oscar Romero (1917–1980), the archbishop of San Salvador, was martyred during the civil war between the government and farmers over land rights. He taught and lived the Gospel through the Church's social teaching, and he spoke out against violence, poverty, and injustice, often using the radio.

Pope John Paul II the Great (1920–2005) was born Karol Wojtyla in Krakow, Poland. He was a playwright, actor, youth minister and chaplain, priest, bishop, philosopher, author, and pope. Two of his plays were made into movies. This Pope has also been called the Great Communicator.

Try to obtain a statement of purpose for each of these types of communications activities.
- Research the media activities of the Bishops' Conference, the local diocese and the parish.

Try to find clear statements or even pastoral plans for these activities. Find out how they are incorporating media with spirituality.

- Research the communications plans of religious communities in the diocese. Contact them and ask if they have a communications director and a communications plan (these communities can carry out any form of apostolate or ministry). How do these religious communities use media to share information about their founder and their unique spiritual charism?

Have the student pairs make the presentations. Afterward, lead a conversation about how understanding of the theology of communication gives impetus and life to these ministries and activities in the Church and the world today. Ask each person to share the one thing that impressed them from these presentations, and what they will remember.

Activity 3: The Theology of Communication and Our Visual Culture

Give each young person a copy of handout 10–A, "Symbolism." The object of this activity is for each person to understand how everyday images and symbols can communicate the nature and presence of God in many places in addition to church. Students can draw symbols freehand, or they can take photos of symbols. They should list the symbol in the left-hand column and then in the right-hand column explain how it communicates something about God to them. After each person has completed this project, have a conversation about how the young people recognized God through various symbols.

Activity 4: Evaluating Religious Communication on Television

Handout 10–B, "Religious Communication via Television and Media Mindfulness," can be used to evaluate any type of communication by religious communities or the Church.

One way to use this tool: begin by inviting each young person to watch a 1-hour religious television program. (This program does not have to be Catholic.) You can tape a religious program and bring it to the class or gathering. Students should use handout 10–B to evaluate the program. Invite the students to share their findings with parents or a significant adult.

Reflective Exercise and Closing Prayer

Obtain a copy of Henri Nouwen's *Behold the Beauty of the Lord: Praying with Icons* (South Bend, IN: Ave Maria Press, 1987) as well as holy cards of Rublev's Trinity. (These cards can be found at the Pauline Book and Media Center nearest you, on its Web site, or through another Catholic book store.) This icon visualizes the self-communicating love of the Trinity and God's self-revelation to us.

Create a quiet environment in a space you have prepared, or a chapel or church. If you can, display a large plaque or picture of the icon. Another option would be to project the image using PowerPoint, which would allow you to include photos of the other people Nouwen refers to.

Read aloud, in whole or in part, the first chapter, "Living in the House of Love," which explains the meaning of the icon as Nouwen helps us contemplate it. Be sure to pause when appropriate, and do not rush through this contemplative experience. Before the conclusion of the chapter, invite the young people to stop and reflect on their relationships with Jesus and their neighbors and to ask forgiveness for sins and failings.

Conclude the prayer service by inviting the group to pray the concluding prayer on handout 10–C, "Canticle of Praise for the Media," alternating stanzas between half of the group and the other. Pray the last stanza together.

Self-Evaluation

Please fill out a copy of handout appendix 6–A, "Self-Evaluation," in this manual.

Cross-Curricular Connections

 History or Church History. Have the students research how Christian Crusaders, Muslems, and Jews used God's word in the Crusades as a rationale for their actions. What role did communication play in how the Crusades began and were promoted? Ask how God's word, God's self-communication to people, is used as a rationale for war and violence today by Christians, Muslems, and Jews?

Discuss this question with the class: What role did communication or the lack of communication play in the Eastern Schism or the Protestant Reformation?

 Art or Art History. Explore with the students how icons, Renaissance masterpieces, and stained-glass windows communicate the Divine to us through symbol, color, line, and subject. How do religious or other fine art works function as symbols that communicate the Divine?

Theology. Explore how theology—that is, "faith seeking understanding"—and mediated communication can facilitate dialogue among peoples. Write a paper comparing the spirituality of Pope John Paul II and Pope Benedict XVI based on each one's coat of arms.

Physical Education. Ask the students to share examples of athletes who seem to reflect a certain spirituality.

Biology. Research brain theory with your students and the scientists who believe we are "wired for God."

Seeing God in the World

Images of God Outside of Church	Their Meaning

Religious Communication via Television and Media Mindfulness

1. What is going on?

What am I seeing or hearing?

What kind of personal and group response seems appropriate?

Religious Communication via Television and Media Mindfulness

What is the producer's world view? How is God portrayed? How does this program or Web site respect religious differences?

2. What is really going on?

What human and Christian values, morals, and social issues are supported or ignored by this program?

3. What difference does it make?

4. What difference can I make?

(This diagram is adapted from *Believing in a Media Culture*, by Gretchen Hailer, Thomas Zanzig, and Marilyn Kielbasa [Winona, MN: Saint Mary's Press, 1996], page 38. Copyright © 1996 by Saint Mary's Press. All rights reserved.)

Canticle of Praise for the Media

May you be praised, Lord God,
for the printed word
bread for our minds,
light for our lives.

We give thanks for the talents and dedication of all
who serve the truth in love,
and for all whose technical and professional skills
make possible the production of books,
newspapers, magazines, and reviews.

We celebrate, Lord,
the modern marvel of television,
which brings into the heart of our homes
the joy and the pain of all human living.
Music, drama, and laughter are shared
in ways undreamed of in the past.

May you be praised, Lord God,
for the radio,
which soars on the wings of the wind
and provides for each nation
an immediate channel for news,
views and entertainment,
and a means of offering to the listening world its
    own distinctive voice.

We celebrate, Lord,
the writers, artists, directors,
and all those whose gifts
light both theater and cinema
and provide audiences
with a heightened awareness
of their human condition.

We celebrate the wonder
of digital communications,
which manifest a new iconography
that link people around the globe
in solidarity of faith, hope, and love.
We thank you, Lord God,
for the unending Pentecost
of your creative Holy Spirit,
which enables your sons and daughters
to be afire with your Truth, Beauty and Goodness.

May the blind see, the deaf hear,
and the poor receive justice
through the proclamation of the Good News via
    today's media.

Together let us rejoice in the God-given talents and
the creative gifts of those who promote the dignity
of the human person,
and who build communion among peoples the
world over
through their dedication and love.

(Based on the writings of Blessed James Alberione,
    in *Canticle of Praise for the Media*, by Sr. Rose
Pacatte. Copyright © by Daughters of Saint Paul.
Used with permission of Pauline Books and Media.
    All rights reserved.)

Appendix 1

Additional Resources

The following resources can familiarize you with current and recent media.

Periodicals

Entertainment Weekly is an economical magazine that covers various forms of media. The reviews are generally good, and it includes current bestseller lists.

Homiletics is a bimonthly ecumenical homiletic guide that follows the common Lectionary. It is contemporary and relevant, providing suggested film clips from popular films each week. A subscription gives both print and online versions. PowerPoint presentations are also available through its Web site.

Telemedium: The Journal of Media Literacy is published by the National Telemedia Council, a professional nonprofit organization promoting media literacy education through partnerships with educators, informed citizens, and media producers across the country.

Visual Parables is an ecumenical quarterly designed to equip Church leaders to engage with film and use it in preaching and teaching. It reviews films in theatrical release, in video formats, and on cable television; it also includes film discussion guides, a devotional column, a column linking film scenes to the common Lectionary, and many other features exploring film, theology, and the Church.

Books

Belknap, Bryan. *Group's Blockbuster Movie Illustrations: Over 160 Clips for Your Ministry!* Loveland, CO: Group Publishing, 2001. This book presents over 160 film clips according to theme as well as Scripture references, cue times to start and end the clips, and questions. It is suitable for teenagers.

——. *Group's Blockbuster Movie Illustrations: The Sequel.* Loveland, CO: Group Publishing, 2003. This book identifies more than 170 clips from mainstream movies for Christian teens.

Beaudoin, Tom. *Consuming Faith: Integrating Who We Are with What We Buy.* Lanham, MD: Sheed and Ward, 2004. Beaudoin places consumerism, a main influence in contemporary American life, firmly on the agenda for consideration of the believing community, and explores how we can respond.

——. *Virtual Faith: The Irreverent Spiritual Quest of Generation X.* San Francisco: Jossey-Bass Publications, 1998. Beaudoin examines Gen-Xers' search for spiritual meaning and the forces and influences that help define this group. Though somewhat dated, the author's approach is useful for understanding youth today.

Brand, Hilary. *Chocolate for Lent*. Boston: Pauline Books & Media, 2002. This is a six-week guide for Lent using the film *Chocolat*.

———. *The Power of Small Choices*. Boston: Pauline Books & Media, 2006. This is a six-week guide for Lent using the films *The Shawshank Redemption* and *Babette's Feast*. The book suggests a clip from each film for each week and also provides Scripture reflections, outlines, notes for the leader and a group guide.

Chaplain, Heather and Aaron Ruby. *Smartbomb: The Quest for Art, Entertainment, and Big Bucks in the Videogame Revolution*. Chapel Hill, NC: Algonquin Books of Chapel Hill, 2005. This is an accessible history of the video game industry and a look at the people who use the games.

Czarnopys, Theresa Santa and Thomas M. Santa, C. Ss. R. *The Internet and the Family*. Liguori, MO: Liguori Publications, 2000. This pamphlet provides helpful rules about the Internet to guide parents and kids.

Davis, Walter T., Gary Dreibelbis, Teresa Blythe, et al. *Watching What We Watch: Prime-Time Television Through the Lens of Faith*. Louisville, KY: Geneva Press, 2001. This resource guide helps teens and adults unpack popular television through the lens of faith.

Detweiler, Craig and Barry Taylor. *A Matrix of Meanings: Finding God in Pop Culture*. Grand Rapids, MI: Baker Academic, 2003. The authors fearlessly survey popular culture and assess its commercial implications from a Christian perspective that can find God in hidden and strange places. It also offers a Christian way to engage in and critique pop culture.

Fields, Doug, and Eddie James. *Videos That Teach*. Grand Rapids, MI: Zondervan, 1999. This book provides "teachable movie moments from seventy-five modern film classics" suitable for use with teenagers. It offers clip selection, themes, reflections, and Scripture references.

———. *Videos That Teach 2*. Grand Rapids, MI: Zondervan, 2002. Offering "teachable movie moments from seventy-five more modern film classics to spark discussion," this book is suitable for use with teenagers. It offers clip selection, themes, reflections, and scripture references.

———. *Videos That Teach 3*. Grand Rapids, MI: Zondervan, 2004. This book provides more of what came in the previous volumes.

Giannetti, Louis. *Understanding Movies* (10th edition). Upper Saddle River, NJ: Prentice Hall, 2005. This is an excellent, accessible text for high school students or anyone who wants to learn more about movies and film criticism.

Jewett, Robert. *Saint Paul at the Movies: The Apostle's Dialogue with American Culture*. Louisville, KY: Westminster John Knox Press, 1993. A New Testament scholar has written an enlightening book about the Greco-Roman world of Paul. A movie enthusiast, Jewett has chosen ten popular movies to illustrate the virtues that Paul holds up to the Roman Empire.

———. *Saint Paul Returns to the Movies: Triumph Over Shame.* Grand Rapids, MI: Eerdmans Publishing, 1999. This sequel is as good as, or perhaps better than, the original.

Johnston, Robert K. *Reel Spirituality: Theology and Film in Dialogue.* Grand Rapids, MI: Baker Academic, 2000. Johnson explores filmmaking as an art form and the theological implications of two hundred movies in a way that helps Christians engage with film culture from an informed, critical perspective.

Kavanaugh, John F. *Following Christ in a Consumer Society (Still): The Spirituality of Cultural Resistance.* Maryknoll, NY: Orbis Books, 2003. Kavanaugh has finessed his original book ten years later, addressing globalization, consumerism, social responsibility, and spirituality.

Leonard, Richard, SJ. *Movies That Matter: Reading Film Through the Lens of Faith.* Chicago: Loyola Press, 2006. The author presents fifty movies that he finds especially meaningful from the perspective of faith. He notes teachable moments for each film and offers a theological and spiritual commentary, followed by three brief questions for reflection. This is an ideal reference for high school teachers.

Levine, John R., et al. *The Internet for Dummies.* Indianapolis: Wiley Publishing, Inc., 2005. This book provides the tools to accomplish basic tasks related to the Internet.

Mahony, Roger M. *Film Makers, Film Viewers, Their Challenges and Opportunities.* Boston: Pauline Books & Media, 1992. Cardinal Mahony of Los Angeles assesses the Catholic's relationship with the entertainment industry. With understanding, wisdom, and insight, he also offers pastoral suggestions for parents and those engaged in ministry.

Malone, Peter, MSC, with Rose Pacatte, FSP. *Lights, Camera . . . Faith! A Movie Lover's Guide to Scripture, Cycle A.* Boston: Pauline Books & Media, 2001. This book provides Scripture readings for each Sunday in dialogue with popular Hollywood films. This is for you and your students; there are parallel books for Cycle B (2002) and Cycle C (2003).

May, John R. *Nourishing Faith Through Fiction: Reflections of the "Apostles' Creed" in Literature and Film.* Lanham, MD: Sheed & Ward, 2001. An American pioneer in cinema studies examines stories that evoke the presence and images of the Trinity, the Creator, the Savior, and the Holy Spirit, the Life-giver. Classic movies and novels are considered in reference to many contemporary movies.

McNulty, Edward. *Praying the Movies: Daily Meditations from Classic Films.* Louisville, KY: Geneva Press, 2001. This book is a collection of thirty-one devotions (one for each day of a month) that connect movies with the spiritual life of moviegoers.

———. *Praying the Movies II. More Daily Meditations from Classic Films.* Louisville, KY: John Knox Press, 2004. Each of these thirty-one devotionals is built around a film scene. Included are related passages from the Old and New Testaments, film synopses and scene descriptions, questions for reflection, hymn suggestions, and closing prayers.

Ogilvy, David. *Ogilvy on Advertising.* New York: Vintage Books, 1983. David Ogilvy has been called the "father of advertising," and this book is now considered a classic, outlining the ideas that formed the premises of contemporary print advertising.

Pacatte, Rose, FSP. *The Nativity Story: A Film Study Guide for Catholics.* Boston: Pauline Books and Media, 2006. This practical three-part study guide for personal and group use takes a whole community catechesis approach to the film with questions for adults, teens, and children for Advent and Christmas.

Pacatte, Rose, FSP, and Peter Malone, MSC. *Lights, Camera . . . Faith! The Ten Commandments*. Boston: Pauline Books & Media, 2006. This book provides scripture readings in dialogue with three films for each commandment: one film for teens and two for young adults and adults. There is a catechetical introduction to each commandment.

Pungente, John, SJ, and Monty Williams, SJ, foreword by John English, SJ. *Finding God in the Dark: Taking the Spiritual Exercises of St. Ignatius to the Movies*. Boston: Pauline Books & Media, 2005. This resource divides the spiritual exercises into fifty-two sessions and discusses a mainstream film for each theme. The introduction includes media literacy application for the faith community.

Romanowski, William D. *Pop Culture Wars: Religion and the Role of Entertainment in American Life*. Downers Grove, IL: InterVarsity Press, 1996. This is a wide-ranging study of entertainment (including cinema), noting the religious traditions hostile to popular entertainment as well as the movements to find the religious values in media and entertainment.

Rodman, George. *Mass Media in a Changing World*. Boston: McGraw Hill, 2006. This media literacy textbook and DVD is up to date as of 2006 and packaged with access to PowerWeb. It is an excellent reference book for teachers and youth ministers.

Smithouser, Bob. *Movie Nights: 25 Movies to Spark Spiritual Discussions with Your Teen*, updated edition. Carol Stream, IL: Tyndale House Publishers, 2005. This book helps teens critically evaluate films through twenty-five highly entertaining movies, and provides Scripture connections as well.

Soukup, Paul. *A Road from Eden: How God Restores Blocked Communication*. Boston: Pauline Books & Media, 2006. This small book explores all the dimensions of communication, offering hopeful and practical solutions to conflict from the family to organizations.

Stoller, Bryan Michael et al. *Filmmaking for Dummies*. Hoboken, NJ: Wiley Publishing, Inc., 2003. This step-by-step guide is accessible and informative.

United States Conference of Catholic Bishops. *The National Directory for Catechesis*. Washington, DC: USCCB, 2005. This book gives exceptional attention to the use of audio visuals in catechesis, catechizing the media, and becoming a critical consumer of media.

Vaux, Sara Anson. *Finding Meaning at the Movies*. Nashville: Abingdon Press, 1999. Vaux offers reflections, critical analysis, and suggestions for conversations on popular movie themes for the Christian audience.

Video

Be sure to prescreen all DVDs and videos for suitability for your group.

Note: If you are unable to acquire any other resources, we recommend that you choose *Scanning Television*, in DVD or video. The clips correspond to every aspect of media literacy education.

Killing Us Softly 3: Advertising's Image of Women with Jean Killbourne. Media Education Foundation, 2002; 34 minutes with an approx. 25-minute interview, not rated. This film is about gender stereotyping in advertising. See the Center for Media Literacy Web site for versions that can be used in high school and nonprofit settings.

The Merchants of Cool with Douglas Rushkoff. PBS *Frontline*, 2001; 60 minutes, not rated. This is an exploration into how corporations market to teens and how a trend becomes "cool."

Scanning Television: 51 Short Videos for Media Literacy Studies DVD, second edition, by John J. Pugente, SJ, and *Teacher's Guide* by Neil Anderson, Kathleen Tyner, and John J. Pungente, SJ. Harcourt Canada and Face to Face Media, Ltd. 2003, not rated. This contains fifty-one copyright-cleared clips and short films on media for media literacy courses, available on video and DVD, with a teacher's guide.

Organizations with Great Web Sites

Whether entirely Web-based or not, these organizations have excellent sites.

CatholicWeb.com is a vast resource of information for catechists and parishes.

Center for Media Literacy is the United States' best Web site on this topic. Find information, downloadables, archived articles, and an online media literacy resource store.

Cornerstone Media provides print and audio resources for teachers, youth ministers, and parents on contemporary music.

FaithStreams.com is a video-on-demand, in English and Spanish, from Faith & Values Media, the nation's largest coalition of Jewish and Christian faith groups dedicated to media production, distribution, and promotion.

The Internet Movie Database provides in-depth information about films and television shows, reviews, ratings, and so on.

SIGNIS, the Vatican-approved World Catholic Association for Communication, has information on Catholic communications globally. The **Catholic Academy for Communication Arts Professionals** is the United States affiliate of SIGNIS; the **Association of Roman Catholic Communicators of Canada** is the Canadian (English-speaking) affiliate.

The United States Conference of Catholic Bishops' Office for Film and Broadcasting has television and film reviews and ratings.

Appendix 2: The Major Themes of Catholic Social Teaching

The Church's social teaching is a rich treasure of wisdom about building a just society and living lives of holiness amidst the challenges of modern society. Modern Catholic social teaching has been articulated through a tradition of papal, conciliar, and episcopal documents. The depth and richness of this tradition can be understood best through a direct reading of these documents. In these brief reflections, we wish to highlight several of the key themes that are at the heart of our Catholic social tradition.

Life and Dignity of the Human Person

The Catholic Church proclaims that human life is sacred and that the dignity of the human person is the foundation of a moral vision for society. Our belief in the sanctity of human life and the inherent dignity of the human person is the foundation of all the principles of our social teaching. In our society, human life is under direct attack from abortion and assisted suicide. The value of human life is being threatened by increasing use of the death penalty. We believe that every person is precious, that people are more important than things, and that the measure of every institution is whether it threatens or enhances the life and dignity of the human person.

Call to Family, Community, and Participation

The person is not only sacred but also social. How we organize our society—in economics and politics, in law and policy—directly affects human dignity and the capacity of individuals to grow in community. The family is the central social institution that must be supported and strengthened, not undermined. We believe people have a right and a duty to participate in society, seeking together the common good and well-being of all, especially the poor and vulnerable.

Rights and Responsibilities

The Catholic tradition teaches that human dignity can be protected and a healthy community can be achieved only if human rights are protected and responsibilities are met. Therefore, every person has a fundamental right to life and a right to those things required for human decency. Corresponding to these rights are duties and responsibilities—to one another, to our families, and to the larger society.

Option for the Poor and Vulnerable

A basic moral test is how our most vulnerable members are faring. In a society marred by deepening divisions between rich and poor, our tradition recalls the story of the Last Judgment (Mt 25:31–46) and instructs us to put the needs of the poor and vulnerable first.

The Dignity of Work and the Rights of Workers

The economy must serve people, not the other way around. Work is more than a way to make a living; it is a form of continuing participation in God's creation. If the dignity of work is to be protected, then the basic rights of workers must be respected—the right to productive work, to decent and fair wages, to organize and join unions, to private property, and to economic initiative.

Solidarity

We are our brothers' and sisters' keepers, wherever they live. We are one human family, whatever our national, racial, ethnic, economic, and ideological differences. Learning to practice the virtue of solidarity means learning that "loving our neighbor" has global dimensions in an interdependent world.

Care for God's Creation

We show our respect for the Creator by our stewardship of creation. Care for the earth is not just an Earth Day slogan, it is a requirement of our faith. We are called to protect people and the planet, living our faith in relationship with all of God's creation. This environmental challenge has fundamental moral and ethical dimensions that cannot be ignored.

Appendix 3

Parents and Media Issues

Parents sometimes have a contentious relationship with entertainment media and popular culture, whose questionable content adds strain to their parenting role. This situation can make it difficult for parents to grasp how the world of entertainment media can be used appropriately in settings where faith formation is ongoing, such as the Catholic school, youth ministry gatherings, or the parish.

The *National Directory for Catechesis* (USCCB, 2005) asserts that the media in themselves are necessary subjects of catechesis, that is, faith formation. The document states that the catechetical plan for a parish "should help people develop their knowledge and skills as viewers, listeners, readers, and users so that they might understand and evaluate the media in the light of the Gospel" (p. 291).

This section will highlight some parenting and media issues and offer strategies to help you develop a media mindfulness connection with the parents and guardians of the young people with whom you work.

Control Is for the Moment; Communication Is for Life

Parents have a golden opportunity to share their values through conversation when they watch film or television with their children and teens—a film or program that deals with a specific value, a challenge to virtue, or one of life's difficulties. Through these discussions, parents may find that their children have more wisdom than they had credited them with. Experiencing age-appropriate media together is an excellent way for family moral education to occur.

Many parents work outside the home and may have little time to watch television and DVDs with children and teens regularly, or to consistently supervise their online activities. To be honest, few parents or adults can absorb too much preschool programming, yet this is the time when parents have the most potential to influence their children to become critical thinkers.

Parents can promote age-appropriate media mindfulness with their children of any age. With younger children, they can talk about how programs are made, how the music makes us feel, the purpose of sound effects, and who makes the programs and why. They can also converse about what stories mean, what advertising and commercials are about, the values that are present (teamwork, kindness, and sharing) and the source of the dramatic conflict: non-Gospel values such as greed, dishonesty, selfishness, and so forth.

One result of solely using "control methods" with media is that when children enter their teens, they realize *what* their parents like or do not like, and often work around these preferences with little understanding of them. Under the "control

134

only" model, young people have no idea *why* their parents like or do not like something because their parents have not communicated their reasons for their choices or media decisions.

Comparing human and Gospel values with media content as they consume media together can help the whole family live these values. In the blockbuster film *Cheaper By the Dozen* (2003, 98 minutes, rated PG), Kate, the mother, confronts her young adult daughter, Lorraine, when she finds her boyfriend staying over in the family home, telling her that this is a problem because their home is rated G! This scene encapsulates the way many parents deal with ratings. Kate does not explain why G-rated behavior is appropriate in a home with so many young children and why her daughter's R- or NC-17-rated behavior does not fit. In fact, it would seem that it's all right with Kate for Lorraine to have sex, just "not in my house." Kate misses a golden opportunity to explain chastity to her daughter and the boyfriend. This confrontation between mother and daughter illustrates control, not communication.

Parents and Their Children's Media Consumption

Information and entertainment media are hot-button issues for many parents. Frequently, parental concerns center on material that is inappropriate for an age-group. These elements—the exposure of body parts, sexual behavior, violence, vulgar language and swearing, and more recently, an awareness of alcohol and drug use and smoking—may or may not be gratuitous. They may be integral to the storyline. To judge media on the basis of these issues alone is called "content analysis" because it does not take the context into account.

A mother was very upset that a Catholic magazine had featured an article that praised the 2004 film *Millions* (98 minutes, rated PG-13) for its Christian themes because of one scene in the movie.

She turned the movie off when a pre-adolescent boy Anthony finds an Internet web site of a woman with a bra on. Not only did the scene show the woman with clothing on, but the mother watching the film never did find out that what follows is perfectly in accord with Catholic teaching. Anthony's little brother, Damien, comes in the room and asks his older brother what breasts are for. His brother explains that women feed their babies with their breasts. Damien, who misses his mother who has died, marvels that his mother once fed him with her own body. The scene was inspiring, not immoral.

With children younger than eight or nine, it is easier for parents to control what they see and how much time they spend on the computer. Much of children's programming is scheduled for the times young children are most likely to watch. Television for pre-teens is scheduled for after-school hours, but pre-teens and teens without jobs often have access to the television and computer at all hours, plus DVDs that they can rent, borrow from their friends, or watch at the homes of their friends when parents are not around. In addition to this easy access, young people are always more interested in activities and programs that are for youth two or three years older than they are.

Television ratings appear on the broadcast cable and satellite channels, yet not all parents take the time to understand what they mean. (See appendix 5, "More Tools for Media Mindfulness" for ways to access information about ratings.) For example, parents may think FV means "family viewing," when it really means "fantasy violence." Confused parents become upset when the show they think is for family has violence, yet the meanings of these ratings are a click away on the computer or printed in the TV guide.

Even though parents have rating systems and programming locks such as the V-chip available to them, some parents do not use them. And of those parents who do use them, many do not take the time to explain to their children *why* some programming is inappropriate or beyond their understanding.

Some parents also fail to realize that even if they think they control what their children have access to at home, young people are influenced by the media culture through their friends and through the visual universe we inhabit.

Clearly, parents need to go beyond responsible control of their children and teens' media consumption. They can actually use media as tools to help form their sons and daughters into discerning Christian men and women.

Looking Beyond the Ratings

Parents may miss an opportunity to talk about the real issue behind inappropriate programming by focusing on the obvious (sex, language, violence, smoking and alcohol, and sometimes drug use) and missing a most insidious danger in media: the creation of artificial needs through advertising. These needs in turn create a sense of entitlement that only having more things will satisfy. Children are then dissatisfied when they cannot have the items advertised. In addition, when commercials and ads rarely show people working and getting their hands dirty, the dream world constructed by entertainment media is reinforced. Parents who recognize the workings of media and then share their own values have the greatest chance of countering the fundamental problem of materialism and consumerism.

However, the single biggest problem with ratings and the mind-set they help create in the culture is that they signal what seems obviously objectionable to the *culture's sensibilities* only. G-rated films, for example, seem innocuous, but more often than not these movies purvey consumerism and materialism through all the toys, soundtracks, and trinkets that are sold along with the film. To miss the consumerism and the creation of false needs in G-rated media, to see only sex and violence with PG-13 and R ratings as problematic, is to miss another major underlying problem with media: how consumerism objectifies the human person. This is not to say, however, that avoiding or critiquing vio-

lence, ridiculing language, or bathroom humor with children of different ages is not appropriate.

All media create chances to talk about prevalent cultural values. "G-rated" is not a comfort zone. The solution is to apply critical thinking skills, informed by Gospel values, to these varied cultural products and learn to choose wisely, whether someone is watching us or not. Through communication, parents can help their children internalize Gospel values in a way that merely controlling media cannot.

Some people decide never to see an R-rated film, and in so doing may choose bathroom humor (PG-13) or boredom because many grown-ups do not want to watch only animated family films. Often R-rated films are more interesting because they wrestle with the dark, light, and gray shades of human experience, and often provide material for our moral imagination to work on. Some scenarios engage our moral imagination so that we can learn the consequences of the choices the protagonist is considering. By putting ourselves in another situation or scenario, we can learn empathy and good judgment. By making a blanket judgment that teenagers can never see an R-rated movie, parents can miss opportunities to talk about powerful human realities and God's action in the world.

Helping Parents Understand Media Mindfulness

When pastoral ministers and educators want to use television or film clips, show movies, or even describe or talk about them, they often encounter fear on the part of the parents. There are several reasons for this. First, parents naturally want to protect their children from every harm, real, potential, or imagined.

Second, they know they are the first teachers of their children and responsible for them, yet the world of popular culture can be easier to deal with through denial or the illusion of control rather than through engagement in it as people of faith. Third, parents either remember what they were like as kids and don't want their children exposed to inappropriate media, or they have forgotten what it was like to be immersed in the culture. Some think that saying "Not in my house!" covers their responsibility. Fourth, parents (and some pastoral ministers) are so negatively conditioned about media that they refuse to use mainstream media in a faith context, or perhaps only G-rated media. Fifth, parents are also conflicted about their personal media use (for example, studies have shown that adults will take time from sleep—but not from TV-watching—to go on the Internet or do e-mail. These parents may themselves struggle to set an example. Sixth, some parents see mainstream entertainment media as a waste of time and believe that school, religious education class, or even youth gatherings are not the places to look at movies, commercials, magazines, and so on. This may be symptomatic of a dichotomy between how people perceive their religious life (Sunday) and everything else they do (the rest of the week).

This guide, therefore, is a way to begin to integrate Sunday with the rest of the week so that religious faith and practice influence our daily lives (our visual, mediated culture-dominated daily lives), and our everyday lives are part of our faith lives.

For all these reasons and more, parents may object to your using media in your ministry. Here are some tips to encourage parents to come on board with your program:

- From the beginning, inform and involve the school or parish leadership in the course. Be sure to obtain necessary permission from them ahead of time.
- Be aware of your parish and diocesan culture, because some bishops permit only G-rated films (or other media forms) to be used in their dioceses. Seek permission ahead of time if this is an issue.
- Notify parents or guardians about your program or event. List the movies and ratings or television clips you intend to use. Attach a permis-

sion form if necessary (see handout appendix 3–A, "Sample Letter for a Media Mindfulness Course," which can be adapted for various situations). Invite parents and guardians to participate, and include a schedule.

- In general, avoid controversial films and those rated R. Please note that an R rating does not mean a movie is bad or immoral; rather, it means that the subject matter and presentation is for those seventeen and older. For example, *Dead Man Walking* is a superb film with Gospel values, yet the subject matter needs parental guidance especially for young teens. *The Insider* is rated R for language, yet the story addresses an important human and social issue, telling how U.S. tobacco companies addicted millions of people to nicotine and covered it up for many years. One can argue that its seriousness does not excuse its bad language but is certainly more important.

- Consider holding a meeting with parents and guardians to announce the course or event and give an overview of media mindfulness from the perspective of good parenting; seek to motivate the parents and welcome their questions, suggestions, and so on. Prepare a handout with the Web address of the Center for Media Literacy so they can seek more information. Give them a copy of handout appendix 3–B, "What Is an Effective and Responsible Catholic Response to Television?" and handout appendix 3–C, "Five Key Questions and Questions to Guide Young Children." You may also order extra copies of this book so that parents may purchase a copy and follow along.

Parents will feel much more comfortable sharing their values about media with their children once they have some tools to use.

Sample Letter for a Media Mindfulness Course

School/Parish Letterhead

[Date]

Dear Parent or Caregiver,

[School, youth group, parish] is planning a mini-course on media mindfulness beginning on [date].

The objective of the course is to help [students / young people] develop critical skills regarding (1) their media choices and (2) making meaning from the entertainment and information media they consume, using the perspective of faith and values. They will learn about each medium, including the Internet, what the Church has to say about the medium, how to critique programs, songs, games, movies, books, etc., and the responsible use of the medium.

During this course [I/we] will use clips from television and several films [and demonstrate video games and play recorded songs], such as:

• [Name of film/rating]

• [Name of film/rating]

• [Name of film/rating]

• [Name of song/game]

You will note that some of the films have an "R" rating; however, the clips used will be appropriate to the subject matter. We will see [name of film/rating] in its entirety.

For your son or daughter to reap the maximum benefit from this course, your support is essential. Therefore [I/we] would like to invite you to a presentation about the course on [day/date/time/place]. At that time, you will be able see the course materials and ask questions as well. Also, from time to time, your teen will bring home activities to share with you; please give your teen some time to explore the activities or issues with you.

Please sign the permission form and return it to me no later than [date] so your teen will be able to participate in the course.

Thank you.

Sincerely,

[Signed and co-signed by the teacher/youth minister/principal/pastor]

--✁

Name of course

Permission form

Dear [your name],

_____ [name of student] has my permission to participate in the mini-course on media mindfulness.

__ I will attend the presentation for parents and caregivers on _____

__ I will not attend the presentation for parents and caregivers on _____

Sincerely,

_____ Parent/Caregiver   Date __/__/__

What Is an Effective and Responsible Catholic Response to Television?

Television, indeed visual messages in all forms, is pervasive in the world today. The responsible Catholic response has these elements:

1. Choose programming wisely, that is, in accord with the human and Gospel values that guide our lives; this presupposes that viewers can articulate these values.

2. Once a person has chosen what to watch, encourage dialogue and questioning of its content, especially the news and commercials.

3. Be involved in the television lives of children and those with whom you share faith, without using television as a baby-sitter.

4. Be able to explain why you choose to watch or not watch a program. Avoid limiting your response to "Not in my house."

5. Even if your family chooses not to own a television, children will be influenced by it through their friends and print advertising. It is essential that children learn at an early age to question what television teaches us.

6. Prioritize your daily activities in a balanced way so that family, spiritual life, school, sports or physical exercise, and charitable activities are at the top of the list.

7. Keep in mind that Catholic social teaching has much to say about television programming and can challenge viewers on many levels. These are some questions based on social justice principles:

- Are people of different races, ages, gender, religious faith, and social condition featured in prime-time television?
- Do comedies respect the dignity of the human person?
- What countries and conflicts are left out of the nightly news?
- Is care for the earth promoted in advertising?
- Does every person in the show have a voice, or is only one point of view presented?

8. Keep in mind that the media makers of tomorrow are in our living rooms, classrooms, and pews today. By teaching media mindfulness skills, you can influence the television industry in years to come.

9. Mentor and financially support Catholics who desire a career in television to integrate their values creatively and artistically into productions.

Five Key Questions to Guide Young Children

This chart takes the "Key Questions" and "Core Concepts" of Media Literacy and adapts them for children.

	Core Concepts	Key Questions	Questions to Guide Children
1	All media messages are "constructed"	Who created this message?	What is this? How is this put together?
2	Media messages are constructed using a creative language with its own rules.	What techniques are used to attract my attention?	What do I see or hear? smell? touch or taste? What do I like or dislike about it?
3	Different people experience the same media messages differently.	How might different people understand this message differently from me?	What do I think and feel about this? What might other people think and feel about this?
4	Media have embedded values and points of view.	What lifestyles, values, and point of view are represented or omitted in this message?	What does this tell me about how other people live and what they believe? Is anything or anyone left out?
5	Media are organized to gain profit and power.	Why was this message sent?	Is this trying to *tell* me something? Is this trying to *sell* me something?

(" Five Key Questions to Guide Young Children" on this handout are from the Center for Media Literacy Web site at *www.medialit.org/reading_room/article623.html*, accessed October 12, 2006.)

Handout Appendix 3–C: Permission to reproduce is granted. © 2007 by Saint Mary's Press.

Appendix 4

Fair Use of Media

Understanding the copyright laws that apply to media is essential to avoid illegal use of film, television, music, and the Internet in media mindfulness education. Laws change, so please check with your school or diocesan procedures or visit the Web site for the United States Copyright Office. If you need help discerning whether you need to ask copyright permission, contact your diocesan media center or Catholic schools office; they should know and support the latest policies.

All information provided in this appendix is accurate as of the date of publication.

Using Feature-Length Films

A Catholic high school teacher has permission to use an authentic copy of a feature-length film in its entirety, without a license, for an educational purpose in the classroom during a regularly scheduled class period. Showing a film in a group setting outside the regularly structured curriculum of an educational institution probably requires a license. Youth ministry programs are not considered educational institutions. As a youth minister, you will need to acquire a license for showing a movie during any sort of parish movie event. High school teachers will need a license to show movies for all events outside of the high school classroom, such as films shown in the lunchroom, an "evening at the movies," or a youth retreat. There are several ways you can obtain permission.

- **The Motion Picture Licensing Corporation/Christian Video Licensing International** can issue an umbrella license for many of the studios. Please call 888-771-2854 or visit the Web site.
- **Swank Motion Pictures** can issue licenses for some films not covered by the MPCC from Miramax and HBO. Please call 800-876-5577.

For all films or studios not covered by the licenses these companies can provide, please contact the studio directly and ask for the licensing or legal department.

Using Television Programs

For educational purposes, within ten days of recording it, a teacher can legally show a broadcast television program he or she has recorded. After that time, the tape must be erased.

If you wish to use an entire television show that is prerecorded on DVD, please contact the production company for permission.

Using Clips from Television and Movies

Film and television clips can be used in an educational setting without a license under a fair-use clause of the federal government. These clips must be brief—no more than 10 percent of the whole film or program.

Using Music

For information about fair use of music, look for the Recording Industry of America guidelines.

Using the Internet

When using any type of information from the Internet—written content, pictures, music, or film clips, for example—please investigate what you can use in an educational setting and what type of permission you will need for use in other settings. Organizations with Web sites often list their permissions process on their home page.

Appendix 5

More Tools for Media Mindfulness

Rating Systems

As part of your work in educating young people and parents about media mindfulness, make sure they are familiar with the rating systems that are used in secular and religious arenas. Look for the Web sites of the following organizations on the Internet.

Television

TV Parental Guidelines Monitoring Board. This organization explains these terms: TV Y, TV Y7, TV7 FV, TVG, TV PG, TV 14, and TV MA.

Video Games

Federal Trade Commission. Here you will find explanations for video game rating abbreviations such as RP, EC, E, E 10+, T, M, and AO.

Movies

Motion Picture Association of America. This organization explains movie rating terms such as G, PG, PG-13, R, and NC-17.

United States Conference of Catholic Bishops' Office for Film and Broadcasting. This office rates movies and assigns them to one of the following categories: A-I, A-II, A-III, L, or O.

Music

Recording Industry of America. This organization uses a Parental Advisory Label that indicates that the music may have explicit content that requires parental discretion.

Ongoing Teacher Training

Center for Media Literacy. This organization has the United States' best Web site on this topic, offering information, downloadables, archived articles, and an online media literacy resource store.

Media Literacy Clearing House. This organization offers numerous ideas for media literacy activities as well as articles about media literacy education.

Pauline Center for Media Studies. This organization offers information and articles on media literacy within the context of faith formation.

Professional Media Literacy Organizations

Alliance for a Media Literate America (AMLA). This is a "national coalition founded in 2001 dedicated to the promotion of media literacy education that encourages hope rather than cynicism, participation rather than passivity, probing discussion rather than rhetorical attacks, healthy skepticism rather than suspicion, and inclusion rather than exclusion." This organization is appropriate for any person interested in media literacy who has a strong faith affinity group.

Association for Media Literacy (AML). This organization is for teachers, librarians, consultants, parents, cultural workers, and media professionals in Canada who are concerned about mass media's influence on contemporary culture.

Canadian Association of Media Literacy Organizations (CAMEO). This organization was founded in 1992. The goal of CAMEO, through its member organizations, is to advocate, promote, and develop media literacy in Canada.

National Association for Catechetical Media Professionals (NACMP). This organization "promotes the development and effective use of media in faith formation throughout Catholic dioceses." While most members are diocesan media librarians or publishers of media for faith formation, this organization is a great resource for catechists and youth ministers.

Appendix 6

Self-Evaluation

Use this tool to evaluate a media mindfulness session or a project such as a film festival.

It is important to assess the lessons you have presented. For media mindfulness activities, we encourage you to use the evaluation format below.

Take a few moments for an "instant replay" of the session you have planned and carried out based on this guide and other sources. If you are working as a team with other adults, you may want to do the evaluation together. Because this is a media mindfulness session, reflect on your awareness of the sounds and images from the session as well as the responses and interaction of the young people.

Sounds. What did you hear that let you know how the session was going?

Images. What did you see that clued you in to how the session was going?

Feelings. How did you feel about the session before, during, and afterward? Did the session meet your expectations? Why or why not? Do you feel it met the expectations of the young people? Why or why not?

Follow-up. Identify elements of the session that you can finesse or change so that your time with young people can be more meaningful.

Acknowledgments

The scriptural quotations contained herein are from the New Revised Standard Version of the Bible, Catholic Edition. Copyright © 1993 and 1989 by the Division of Christian Education of the National Council of the Churches of Christ in the United States of America. All rights reserved.

The excerpt on page 7 is from "Media Literacy: A National Priority in a Changing World," by Sr. Elizabeth Thoman, CHM, and Tessa Jolls, in *American Behavioral Scientist*, volume 48, number 1, September 2004.

The quotation on page 8 is from *Screening Images: Ideas for Media Education*, second edition, by Chris Worsnop (Mississauga, Ontario Canada: Wright Communications, 1999), page ix, ISBN 0-9697954-2-4. Used with permission.

"Five Key Questions" and "Five Core Concepts" on page 8 are taken from "MediaLit Kit" on the Center for Media Literacy Web site, *www.medialit.org/pdf/mlk/14A_CCKQposter.pdf*, accessed October 12, 2006. Copyright © 2005 by the Center for Media Literacy. Used with permission.

The excerpts on pages 9 and 63 are from the introduction of Pope Pius XII's encyclical letter *On Motion Pictures, Radio, and Television (Miranda Prorsus)*, at *www.vatican.va/holy_father/pius_xii/encyclicals/documents/hf_p-xii_enc_08091957_miranda-prorsus_en.html*, accessed October 12, 2006.

The quotation on page 15 is from "Message of the Holy Father for the XVIII World Communications Day," number 2, at *www.vatican.va/holy_father/john_paul_ii/messages/communications/documents/hf_jp-ii_mes_24051984_world-communications-day_en.html*, accessed October 12, 2006.

The list "What Media Literacy Is *Not*" on page 16 is from the Center for Media Literacy Web site, *www.medialit.org/reading_room/article380.html*, accessed October 12, 2006.

The media mindfulness wheel on pages 16 and 17 and on handouts 1–B, 2–B, 3–B, 4–B, 5–B, 6–B, 7–B, 8–B, 9–B, and 10–B is adapted from and the information on handout 3–A is from *Believing in a Media Culture*, by Gretchen Hailer, Thomas Zanzig, and Marilyn Kielbasa (Winona, MN: Saint Mary's Press, 1996), pages 22, 38 (handouts), and 49, respectively. Copyright © 1996 by Saint Mary's Press. All rights reserved.

The quotation on page 17 is from *The Divine Milieu: An Essay on the Interior Life*, by Pierre Teilhard de Chardin, SJ (New York: Harper and Row, 1957), page 66. Copyright © 1957 by Editions du Seuil.

The excerpts by Pope John Paul II on pages 18 and 29 are from the apostolic Letter *The Rapid Development of the Holy Father John Paul II to Those Responsible for Communications*, number 2, at *www.vatican.va/holy_father/john_paul_ii/apost_letters/documents/hf_jp-ii_apl_20050124_il-rapido-sviluppo_en.html*, accessed October 12, 2006.

The first excerpt on page 29 is from the pastoral instruction "*Aetatis Novae*, On Social Communications on the Twentieth Anniversary of *Communio et*

Progressio," number 12, at *www.vatican.va/roman_curia/pontifical_councils/pccs/ documents/rc_pc_pccs_doc_22021992_aetatis_en.html,* accessed October 12, 2006.

The quotation and the third excerpt on page 29 and the quotation on page 134 are from *National Directory for Catechesis,* by the United States Conference of Catholic Bishops (USCCB) (Washington, DC: USCCB, 2005), pages 105, 16, and 291, respectively. Copyright © 2005 by the USCCB.

The quotation by Nancy Kerrigan on page 38 is taken from an article on the *Washington Post* Web site, "Kerrigan Off the Ice Doesn't Seem Half as Nice," by Kim Masters, at *www.washingtonpost.com/wp-srv/sports/longterm/olympics1998/ history/timeline/articles/time_030494.htm,* accessed October 12, 2006.

The statement about Michael Jordan on page 38 is paraphrased from the article "Nike Campaign Strikes at Firm's Record in Asia," by the Inter-Press Agency and found at the Boycott Nike Web site, *vietgate.net/~nike/nikeipc.htm,* accessed October 12, 2006.

The statistics on page 40 on the effects on youth of the advertising of alcohol are from the report "Youth Exposure to Alcohol Advertising in Magazines, 2001 to 2004: Good News, Bad News," page 2, on the Center of Alcohol Marketing and Youth Web site, *camy.org/research/mag0506/,* accessed October 12, 2006.

The excerpt on page 41 is taken from "Pontifical Council for Social Communications *Ethics in Advertising,*" number 23, at *www.vatican.va/roman_curia/ pontifical_councils/pccs/documents/rc_pc_pccs_doc_22021997_ethics-in-ad_en.html,* accessed October 12, 2006.

The "treatment of bedrooms" quotation on page 62 is from "The Motion Picture Production Code of 1930 (Hays Code)," found at the ArtsReformation.com Web site, *www.artsreformation.com/a001/hays-code.html,* accessed October 12, 2006.

The second excerpt on page 63 is from "Decree on the Media of Social Communications *Inter Mirifica,* Solemnly Promulgated by His Holiness Pope Paul VI," number 14, at *www.vatican.va/archive/hist_councils/ii_vatican_council/documents/ vat-ii_decree_19631204_inter-mirifica_en.html,* accessed October 12, 2006.

The excerpts about pornography on page 64 are from *Pornography and Violence in the Communications Media: A Pastoral Response,* by the Pontifical Council for Social Communications, numbers 9, 10, and 11, at *www.vatican.va/roman_curia/ pontifical_councils/pccs/documents/rc_pc_pccs_doc_07051989_pornography_en.html,* accessed October 12, 2006.

"Ten Steps for Planning a Youth Film Festival" on pages 65–66 is from *Guide to Planning In-House Film Festivals in Ten Easy Steps: A Media Education Opportunity,* by Rose Pacatte, FSP (Boston: Pauline Books and Media, 2000), pages 18–19. Copyright © 2000 by the Daughters of Saint Paul. Used with permission.

The activity "Frame It!" on handout 5–A is adapted from "Frame It," by Sr. Rose Pacatte, in *My Friend,* October 2005, page 25, illustrated by Virginia Helen Richards and D. Thomas Halpin. Copyright © 2005 by Daughters of Saint Paul. Used with permission.

The description of radio on page 72 and information about the MP3 player on page 73 are from Wikipedia: The Free Encyclopedia Web site, *en.wikipedia.org*, accessed October 12, 2006.

The excerpt about music by Pope Pius X on page 75 is from *Instruction on Sacred Music (Tra le Sollecitudini)*, number 5, found at *www.adoremus.org/TraLeSollecitudini.html*, accessed October 12, 2006.

The Census Bureau statistics on television on page 82 are from the 1960 U.S. Census, on the U. S. Census Bureau Web site, *www.census.gov/Press-Release/www/releases/archives/facts_for_features_special_editions/001702.html*, accessed October 12, 2006.

The quotation by Archbishop John P. Foley on page 85 is from Zenit: The World Seen from Rome Web site, *www.zenit.org/english/visualizza/phtml?sid=85918*, accessed October 12, 2006.

The description of electronic games on page 94 is from *"Video Game Types Defined,"* by Don Lee on the Consumers Electronic Net Web site, *games.consumerelectronicsnet.com*, accessed October 12, 2006.

The Ed Bradley interview on pages 95–96 is from "Can a Video Game Lead to Murder?" at the CBS News Web site, *www.cbsnews.com*, accessed October 12, 2006. Copyright © MMV, CBS Worldwide, Inc.

The excerpt on page 96 and the quotations on page 117 are from *On the Means of Social Communication (Communio et Progressio*, 1971), by the Order of the Second Vatican Council, numbers 52 and 11, at *www.vatican.va/roman_curia/pontifical_councils/pccs/documents/rc_pc_pccs_doc_23051971_communio_en.html*, accessed October 12, 2006.

The excerpt by Pope John Paul II on page 100 is from "Message of the Holy Father for the XXIV World Communications Day," at *www.vatican.va/holy_father/john_paul_ii/messages/communications/documents/hf_jp-ii_mes_24011990_world-communications-day_en.html*, accessed October 12, 2006.

The excerpt about pornography on page 107 is from the United States House of Representatives statement of Rep. Henry A. Waxman, "Hearing on Stumbling into Smut: The Alarming Ease of Access to Pornography on Peer-to-Peer Network," March 13, 2003, at *www.democrats.reform.house.gov*, accessed October 12, 2006.

The excerpts on pages 109–110 are from *The Church and Internet* by the Pontifical Council for Social Communications, numbers 1, 4, 6, 7, 12, 12, 10, 17, 1, 11, and 12, respectively, at *www.vatican.va/roman_curia/pontifical_councils/pccs/documents/rc_pc_pccs_doc_20020228_church-internet_en.html*, accessed October 12, 2006.

The excerpt on page 116 and the quotation on page 118 are from *The Catholic Faith Handbook for Youth (CFH)*, by Brian Singer-Towns et al. (Winona, MN: Saint Mary's Press, 2004), page 425. Copyright © 2004 by Saint Mary's Press. All rights reserved.

The quotation by Fr. Bernard R. Bonnot on page 117 is from VLCFF @ UD > Church and Communication (Test) > Session 4 on the University of Dayton Web site, *www.udayton.edu/~vlc/courses/*, accessed October 12, 2006.

The excerpt from Vatican II on page 117 is from *Pastoral Constitution on the Church in the Modern World* (*Gaudium et Spes*, 1965) promulgated by His Holiness Pope Paul VI, number 1, at *www.vatican.va/archive/hist_councils/ii_vatican_council/documents/vat-ii_cons_19651207_gaudium-et-spes_en.html*, accessed October 12, 2006.

The excerpt on page 118 is from "Apostolic Letter *Novo Millennio Ineunte* of His Holiness Pope John Paul II to the Bishops, Clergy, and Lay Faithful at the Close of the Great Jubilee of the Year 2000," number 43, at *www.vatican.va/holy_father/john_paul_ii/apost_letters/documents/hf_jp-ii_apl_20010106_novo-millennio-ineunte_en.html*, accessed October 12, 2006.

The information in "The Church and Communication in the United States Since Vatican II" on page 119 is derived from a speech by Sr. Elizabeth Thoman to UNDA-USA in 1986 and from notes made from a personal conversation with her by the author.

"Canticle of Praise for the Media" on handout 10–C is from *Canticle of Praise for the Media*, by Sr. Rose Pacatte, based on the writing of Bl. James Alberione. Copyright © by the Daughters of Saint Paul. Used with permission.

The material on handout appendix 2–A is from *Sharing Catholic Social Teaching: Challenges and Directions, Reflections of the U. S. Catholic Bishops*, by the USCCB (Washington, DC: USCCB, 1999), pages 4–6. Copyright © 1999 by the USCCB. Used with permission.

"Five Key Questions to Guide Young Children" on handout appendix 3–C are from the Center for Media Literacy Web site, *www.medialit.org/reading_room/article623.html*, accessed October 12, 2006.

To view copyright terms and conditions for Internet materials cited here, log on to the home pages for the referenced Web sites.

During this book's preparation, all citations, facts, figures, names, addresses, telephone numbers, Internet URLs, and other pieces of information cited within were verified for accuracy. The authors and Saint Mary's Press staff have made every attempt to reference current and valid sources, but we cannot guarantee the content of any source, and we are not responsible for any changes that may have occurred since our verification. If you find an error in, or have a question or concern about, any of the information or sources listed within, please contact Saint Mary's Press.

Endnote Cited in a Quotation from a Document Copyrighted by the USCCB

1. S. IOAN. CHRYS., *De consubstantiali, contra Anomoeos*: P.G., 48, 810.